THE
POMEGRANATE
KING

ESSAYS

NISHTA J. MEHRA

THE POMEGRANATE KING: ESSAYS
2013 © Nishta Jaya Mehra
All rights reserved.
Interior design by Natasha Fondren
Cover design & interior artwork by Allie Mounce

THE
POMEGRANATE KING

ESSAYS

 for my parents

THE POMEGRANATE KING: ESSAYS

Author's Note
The essays in this collection are free-standing but closely related.
They were designed to be read in the order presented here.

"I once heard the Master say 'If you haven't yet faced yourself,
you will when the time comes to mourn your parents.'"

–The Analects

1

Mixed

Ilet my Southern accent go in college. And by "let go," I mean, "deliberately un-cultivated." A few weeks of being asked "Where are you *from*?" and "What kind of accent is *that*?" and I was ready to un-mark myself, strip my voice of what had begun to feel like a flashing neon sign of embarrassing otherness. My accent wasn't the right kind of different, wasn't the kind you could parade flirtatiously at a dorm room party; "I'm from Tennessee" hardly connotes sexy or exotic.

You wouldn't think they'd have much room to talk about funny accents in Houston, Texas, where I received my undergraduate education, but an ivory tower is an ivory tower no matter where it's built; we were all trying so hard to be impressive that I still felt self-conscious. There are plenty of smart Southerners, but a Southern accent doesn't sound smart to most people. I wanted to be taken seriously, so I changed my voice. I watched my modulation, caught myself when vowels threatened to elongate of their own accord. After a while, people could no longer guess where I was from, and I liked that. I thought it made me cosmopolitan, as if I might be from anywhere, unable to be push-pinned on any mental map, mysterious brown girl of indeterminate origin.

But I could only hide in ambiguity for so long. We have a saying where I'm from, about the resurgence of native accents—if you're "drinkin', cheatin', lyin', or cryin'," it will come back with a vengeance. Or, in my case—if you're on the phone in your dorm room, talking to your high school friends. My roommates were forever trying to imitate the drawl of my "Love you! Bye!" which came out more like *"Luvvvv yewww! Baiiiiii!"* Resistance, it seemed, was futile.

And really, the glamour of anonymity was short-lived, transforming instead into a kind of sadness at having lost a distinguishing characteristic. Maybe I sounded like a hick, but at least I sounded like I was from somewhere. By the time college graduation rolled around, I was moving linguistically in the reverse, attempting to bring back what I had purposely lost. Because the reality is, I was born in Memphis, Tennessee. I am a Southern girl: wholly so, fully so, undeniably so, and I won't ever be anything else.

When you meet someone for the first time, it's customary to inquire, "Where are you from?" I, of course, answer "Memphis," which is the truth, but it confuses people. They usually have something else in mind when they ask "Where are you from?" of me. Memphis is not the answer people want, or at least, it is not the answer they expect. Their faces betray quizzical expressions, which in turn confuse *me* until I remember what they see when they look at me. *Oh right*, I think, *I'm brown.*

See, what most people are actually asking me when they politely inquire "Where are you from?" is "What kind of brown are you?" So when I respond "Memphis," they think I must be disingenuous or slow-witted; at times, they even laugh. "No, no, where is your *family* from?" they'll continue kindly, leaning in, emphasizing the word "family" in the hope that I'll become clued into what they really want to know. And indeed, by this point, I have figured out what they're asking; depending on my perceived obnoxiousness of the asker, I'll let them squirm a while or rescue them with the standard line, "My family's from India, but I was born in the States." This will satisfy their curiosity about my color, the same curiosity that drives people to find out the gender of the fat-and-bald baby in the stroller before them.

Generally, this doesn't bother me; there truly is no good way to ask about someone's color, and people mostly mean well. But there are times when I wish my initial answer were enough, because Memphis *is* where I'm from, where my family is, the place my mother has lived longer than any other place, where my father would still be living were he alive, the place I am referring to when I use the word "home."

I am visiting my mom in the days between Christmas and New Year's. She is so happy I am here; she started cooking for this visit weeks ago. It is customary for me to tease her whenever I'm here by peeking into her not one, but two! refrigerators and giving her a hard time about the unbelievable wealth of food she has acquired and prepared for my stay.

"How much do you think I can eat, woman?"

"Hush up," she'll say, but she likes it.

When I return one morning from the gym, mom reports that our next-door neighbor Meredith called while I was away. Meredith and her husband Tom have lived next door since my parents moved into this house; they have known me since I was eighteen months old, and they are more like my family than next-door neighbors. I call them "Uncle Tom" and "Meredith Aunty," the way my parents taught me; I consider their children my older siblings, and their grandchildren my nieces and nephew. In elementary school, when it was Grandparents' Day and mine were all dead or in India, Meredith's parents came as my surrogates. Tom sent me a dozen roses for my sixteenth birthday and always kisses me on the cheek when I see him. He continuously checks in on my mother—she has lived alone since my father's death in 2006—helps with her taxes, invites her out for dinner with the family, calls if he sees a strange car in the driveway, or if Mom's garage is open for what seems like an unusual period of time.

Meredith and Tom were present at my college graduation, having flown down to Texas even though their second grandchild had just been born. Being out to them was nearly as terrifying as being out to my own parents. They have seen me through practically every stage of my life and yet still, on this morning, when Meredith has called for me to come over and say hi and grab my Christmas present (which I can guarantee will be an obscenely generous gift card to a high-end women's clothing store, since they insist on spoiling me even though I am no longer a kid and now pushing thirty), my Mom eyes me in my sweaty gym clothes, cocks her head, and says "You're not going like that, are you?"

I laugh. "No, mom, don't worry. I'll shower and change."

"Okay, good. Because you know what they say..." She grins and I know what's coming, and chime in so we can recite my hometown's unspoken rule in unison: "Smart is good, but smart and pretty is better."

I was raised in an upper-middle class family below the Mason-Dixon line, which means I have very pointed opinions about very particular things: a woman's toenails should always be painted, thank-you notes are a must and should be handwritten, preferably on monogrammed stationery, buttermilk should be used where biscuits, pancakes, and cornbread are concerned, and clucking your tongue and adding "Bless her heart!" to the end of any piece of gossip keeps it from actually being gossip.

Often, I forget how peculiar and distinctive my little set of social norms can seem to others; not everyone was raised this way. My partner Jill, for example, was also raised in the South, but in a decidedly blue-collar household, which means her rules pertain more to hunting, fishing, canning, and self-sufficiency than gentility. Food is our common ground—cornbread, fried okra, grits—but we run into little gaps in our other behaviors and have learned to compromise and shift, self-identify snobbery or disdain. She'll sign the tasteful, custom-embossed "Jill & Nishta" thank-you notes if I write them, and I've learned not to throw anything, no matter how worthless it seems to me, away without asking.

Jill is at least familiar with the quirks of my upbringing; they are not new to her, even if she doesn't share them. But for those who are strangers to the South, it can all seem overwhelming, even insane. Not long ago, I astonished the heck out of my friend Benjamin—he's a Yankee, bless his heart—when I tried to explain the necessity of and principles behind the hostess gift.

"You can't go over to someone's home for the first time empty-handed," I insisted. "A nice bottle of wine is standard, or the host's liquor of choice, if you know it. Should you be unable to match in expenditure the quality to which your host is likely accustomed, an edible gift will work: a bag of spiced nuts, a tin of cookies, preferably homemade, but only if you are good at these kinds of things. If all else fails, spring for some nice flowers—never roses—and have them wrapped in paper, it's classier than plastic."

It isn't as if these things are written down, although I imagine Emily Post has them covered in a chapter or two, and it isn't as if anyone ever sat me down and taught them to me, though there are Junior Cotillions that exist for the sole purpose of grooming young ladies and gentlemen. In my case, these codes of behavior were simply the water I grew up swimming in; resist them though I may (and as I did, for a time), the genteel trappings of my native land are mine. I believe in them, even though I know they are ridiculous. For years, I bucked against the fact that I couldn't seem to quit them, until I finally realized that I wouldn't want to. They are my birthright, my ritual, my tradition.

I tried to explain all of this to Ben. He just shook his head and said, "You Southern women sure are complicated."

St. Mary's Episcopal School for girls was founded in 1847, an academically rigorous prep school steeped in pomp and circumstance, which the outsider may judge but the insider understands. We graduated in white dresses, carrying bouquets of flowers and wearing circlets of matching roses and baby's breath on our heads, kindergarten flower girls marching in front of us like a groom-less wedding. Of course, these graduation dresses, though they look a lot like dresses one might get married in, cannot be recycled for one's *actual* wedding, because that would just be tacky. Fun fact: one of my close friends graduated in a dress made—honest to goodness—from her grandmother's old lace curtains.

I know this world. I spent twelve mostly happy years at St. Mary's; I graduated with honors, was active in community service, Mock Trial, the student-led Honor Council, the Fine Arts Club. My senior yearbook superlative was "All American Ethnic Girl." I know which polo shirts to buy, the way one's hair should be carefully pulled back into a ponytail but not completely smoothed, which nail polish colors are acceptable for toes, and which for fingernails, how to assemble the proper William Sonoma registry, the correct Sunday brunch components, what constitutes acceptable topics for cocktail party chit-chat, and how to tie a birthday present bow. My mother calls me "white girl" when she wants to get my goat.

"Honey, are you mixed?"

It was a question I had never been asked before, let alone in a drive-through line by a complete stranger holding out the change for mine and my mother's order. Backyard Burger is Memphis' homegrown hamburger franchise, and they make a pretty decent drive-through burger for the money. One taste of their thick-cut waffle fries takes me right back to the feeling of a new driver's license and Saturday afternoons. My mom, the vegetarian, loves them for the flavorful vegetarian patties which they cook, considerately, on a separate grill.

At first I thought the drive-through attendant had asked "Do you want ketchup with that?" because her tone was so glib, as if she questioned each customer about the origins of their skin color, as if it were company policy, like saying "Have a nice day!" even when you don't really mean it. I didn't even understand the question at first, let alone comprehend that I might be legitimately offended by it. Instead, I looked up at my questioner's full, dark-skinned face, said "What?" and listened as she repeated her question.

"Oh...um, no. I'm Indian," I answered finally, too well-trained to blow her off—one does not match rudeness with rudeness—but utterly unable to compose an appropriate response. What is the appropriate response in a situation like that, anyway? To turn snobby or cold would reify the very social color strata that likely led to this awkward question-and-answer session in the first place.

I continued out of habit, to clarify that I didn't mean the kind of Indian that kids stereotypically pantomime for backyard play: "I mean, my family's from India. My parents are." I saw her glance at my mother, who has been mistaken for or assumed to be all of the following ethnicities at least once: Greek, Russian, Italian, Korean, Native American, Chinese, Mexican, Caucasian. I, on the other hand, have my father's unmistakably dark brown skin, made browner by my penchant for sunshine. My skin is as dark or darker than several African-American friends of mine. I understood what this woman was seeing: in the world of Memphis, where there is only black or white, I looked like the daughter of a white mother and a black father.

When I counteracted that assumption, though, and proved myself to be something else, outside the categories of Memphis black or white, the woman's demeanor changed. Her body language, which had been imposing and superior, softened, and her tone became deferential.

"Oh," she said. "Oh. 'Cause you sure do have the prettiest skin."

CONTINUE THE CONVERSATION

nes my
new in
e joints
ng as I
iceable

amount. Without trying. And I can never shake the feeling I'm being eyed with suspicion by black women, because it's clear that I am not from their world. I may put pepper sauce in my greens, and be able to keep up with the bantering talk, but no matter how dark my skin gets, no one is fooled; I have come from the white world.

When I was growing up, Memphis was two distinct worlds, a shockingly segregated relic, a step back in time. By now, the city has found its way to Farmers Markets, school reform, inventive cuisine, even a Whole Foods, but most neighborhoods, schools, churches, parks, and barbecue joints still remain split, black or white. Political votes are, with rare and very recent exception, made on the basis of race. A friend of mine recently put it this way: "We may work together, but we don't have each other over for dinner." The city is just beginning to have conversations about its separateness—very hard, very tricky conversations that are made even more difficult by the Southern penchant for dodging the speaking of unpleasant things.

When I return for weddings, holidays, and the like, I rediscover a curious phenomenon; I will, at some point in my visit to Memphis, be the only non-white person in the room. Or rather, the only non-white *guest*, as dark faces at country clubs and restaurants tend to be employees.

This is a feat that would be impossible to imagine in Houston, where I live now, but it's entirely possible to spend your whole Memphis life inside one circle of color or the other. For me to do that, I'd have to go all the way to India, yet in my hometown it isn't unusual, isn't even noticed. White people hang out with white people, black people with black people. The self-segregation takes itself right down to the debutante balls—which still exist, by the way, as the means by which one is "officially introduced to society," while wearing a virginal white dress, of course. There's a ball for the black girls and a ball for the white girls. So, then, where does the brown girl go?

Because I grew up outside the city proper, I learned, as a teenager, to travel within the city limits to shop for makeup. In lily-white suburbia, the darkest shade my Target carried was "tan"—not so helpful to me. As a kid, I attended many an elementary-school birthday party at country club pools, the only non-Caucasian classmate invited and the only non-white guest in sight. I could see the African-American women folding towels and cleaning chairs eyeing me as if to say, "Child, what are you doing here?" As someone who chose teaching English as a profession, my first exposure to irony was at those very parties, watching dozens of white men and women lying on their towels in the sun, soaking in the full power of their privilege while trying their damndest to make their skin as dark as mine.

Please note: the same companies that sell self-tanning lotions and bronzers here in America sell "whitening" or "lightening" creams and face-washes in India. My fair-skinned mother was teased mercilessly while growing up in India, out of jealousy over her complexion. The older girls at her parochial school called her "Macbeth," strange insult conjured with the weirdest Western name they knew.

To this day, if my mother sent a photograph of me to certain relatives in India, comments would be made about how dark I've gotten, tsk tsk, my mother shouldn't let me run around so much outside in the sun, how will she ever find someone for me to marry? But that's a whole other kettle of fish besides.

Eventually I discovered that "*Steel Magnolias* Revisited" was not the only way to live. (The film was standard weekend sleepover fare and I can still recite most of it from memory.) Around the age of sixteen, I started hanging out with the theatre kids, and through them, I met and hung out with kids who went to—gasp!—public school. I cut my hair short. I wore jeans with holes in them: not the strategically placed and mechanically formed tears that high-end boutiques seem to think they can charge more for, but the kind I frayed myself. With scissors. While listening to the Indigo Girls. I even went to see "The Rocky Horror Picture Show" at midnight.

Then I kissed a girl, which wasn't at all part of my measured rebellion—in fact, it caught me completely off guard. I just fell in love, the kind of first love many people have their senior year of high school: glorious, confusing, wonderful, and not without its fair share of drama. But within my relationship, I found the other side of things—across the railroad tracks (literally, I had to cross them to get to my girlfriend's house), a rebellious anti-Memphis which stuck its middle finger out at the plaid and the argyle, which drank lots of coffee and put bumper stickers on its cars, something WASPs never do.

Surprisingly enough, becoming a lesbian was the best thing I ever did for my social life; my girlfriend and I were invited to every weekend party, and I got to know classmates who had previously seemed way too intimidating. I suppose nothing was as intimidating anymore as my having abandoned ship, forgoing social graces, and doing my own thing.

It's freeing at first for a perfectionist to suddenly find that little is expected of her. When the gentility views you as a terribly uncouth heathen, you can then in turn shock them with your ability to slip back into their world undetected, playing the "good girl" part you were raised to play. In this way, I became a kind of cultural double agent, visitor in two diametrically opposite worlds.

As time passed and my parents moved through various stages of freaking out over my sexuality, Memphis-as-I-had-known-it began to move farther and farther away, like a life I was leaving behind and deliberately waving farewell to, all white-picket-fenced and proper, thick, ecru stationery, babies in smocked jumpers. On visits home from college, I flaunted the fact that I had made a life away from Southern puppet strings, showing up with dangerously short hair, tattoos, a nose ring, and an attitude to match. But I still loved my Memphis world too much write it off entirely, and so I would perform the obligatory dress-and-pony show, hiding my tattoos, styling my hair, shaving my legs, unable to really admit to myself (let alone anyone else) how much I enjoyed being back in my native milieu. When I returned to the very diverse world of college, I made fun of Memphis' silly, old-fashioned traditions. When in Memphis, I bemoaned the fact that my college compatriots thought that jeans without holes in them constituted "dressed up" and were not bred to write thank-you notes as I had been.

Being a double agent is risky. There is only so much compartmentalizing you can do before your very sense of self begins to break. Though I had left it, Memphis was still the place where I learned everything first, and it forever echoed in the background of my life, a life I felt certain would never measure up. I hadn't done what was expected of me; I didn't have little girls to send to St. Mary's, or a husband who wears Madras plaid shorts in the summer and obsessive college football loyalties in the fall. That life, so stereotypical, so plebian as it seemed on the one hand, was somehow intoxicatingly compelling as I felt it become inaccessible to me. I visited Memphis and the happiness of my "other" life, queer and multi-colored as a Benetton ad, would dwarf under the weight of what I did not have, of what I thought it would be easier if I *did* have, even though I did not want it. A split, crack and fissure, two different selves.

I have biracial friends whose features are such that they can "pass" for white. Now I may be "the whitest brown girl" that anyone has ever met, but the body I'm housed in is still undeniably brown. When *I* pass, it looks like this: I am back in town and at the bookstore, dressed in appropriately cute clothes, with my hair styled and make-up on and I run into an acquaintance who hasn't yet heard through the grapevine about my "alternative lifestyle" and I don't have energy nor do I want to risk the potential horror of *really* answering the question "How have you been?," so I let myself lie, or at least leave certain things out, and find that I pass respectably for the happy, heterosexual hometown girl, a different kind of play-pretend.

My friends Kate and Stephen are the quintessential Memphis couple. They have the big, beautiful house with a giant fig tree in the backyard, the two beautiful blond-haired and blue-eyed children, the predictably preppy wardrobe and the very Southern accents I tried to rid myself of in college. They are the idealized life I have finally learned to let go of. They are, and I say this with the utmost love and respect, the whitest people I know.

We are sort of sideways friends, our closeness having developed over a long period time. Kate graduated from St. Mary's seven years before I did, then came back to teach a World Religions class. I was her student my junior year, and thanks to my fortuitously-assigned locker (directly outside her office), we got to know each other fairly well over the course of that year—as close as the teacher-student designation would allow. Then she and Stephen, newlyweds, moved to the Washington D.C. area so that Kate could attend seminary in Virginia.

We kept up in touch, seeing each other when both of us were in Memphis over the holidays; I got to know Stephen a bit on the occasions when the three of us would have dinner together. Gradually, we become more and more balanced, friends without disclaimer, so much so that Kate and Stephen asked me to spend my summer in Memphis, living in the upstairs of their house and acting as a sort of fairy godmother to the twins. "We're thinking we could use an extra pair of hands. There's no one else we would ask."

I had the summer free, sandwiched between two years of my Master's program, plus the requisite love for my friends and for babies. So the three of us, plus twins and a speckled dog, became a family for a little while, cooking dinner, doing dishes, managing feedings and diaper changes, and celebrating little victories—like mustering the mental wherewithal to play a game of Scrabble, discovering a new favorite bottle of red wine under $12, John's heat rash dissipating, Stephen's backyard figs ripening, and Katherine being able to fit into pre-pregnancy pants.

During the fall that followed, I remember a phone conversation with Kate as the boys were approaching their baptism date. There was some fear on the part of the boys' grandmothers that the strapping young infants might grow too quickly, making it impossible for them to wear the family baptismal gowns. Luckily, John and Henry held back just enough to allow them to be squeezed into their lacy heirlooms—John into the same gown that his father, aunts, & uncles had worn; Henry into one in which he had been preceded by his mother, aunt, and cousin. I don't think anyone is clear on how or why frilly white dresses and knit, beribboned booties became requisite for entering the communion of Christians, but you just don't argue about these things, not where I'm from.

I am the twins' unofficial godmother. Unofficial because, in the Episcopal church, you have to be a baptized Christian to qualify for the role of godparent, which makes sense. Still, it would have been pretty great to stand up there on the altar with Kate and Stephen while Stephen's father (who, like Kate, is an Episcopal priest) commended his grandsons into the care of their godparents, the community of the faithful, and Jesus. But I am used to these limits of belonging and not belonging. Twelve years as a Hindu in an Episcopal school creates a complicated matrix.

My parents sent me to St. Mary's because it promised a great education; they were undeterred by the school's religious affiliation, my mother herself having been educated by Roman Catholic nuns in India. And while the household I was raised in was clearly Hindu, my interest in the world of Anglicanism was never discouraged. I made an eager Bible class student, crowding the felt board where Mrs. Williams would reenact stories from Jesus' life, but I was also attentive to the stories of my tradition, reading from our holy books on weekends. When the houses in my neighborhood began to sprout Halloween décor, I learned to wait until our holiday of Diwali had passed before we would cobweb our front porch. I skipped lunch when fasting during Hindu holy weeks, and gave up chocolate and Diet Coke with my Christian friends for Lent.

Visiting home still requires a good deal of prep work. Going back means painting toenails, packing dresses and "cute" shoes, tying on the bows and laying out the jewelry: standard Memphis procedure. Happy hour attire in Houston would barely pass for appropriate grocery store wear in my hometown. Far worse was graduate school in Tucson, desert hippie capital of the Southwest; I wanted to hand out gift certificates for pedicures and hair cuts everywhere I went.

"Do I contradict myself?," Whitman would ask. Memphis' by-all-appearances culture is no longer my only measurement for how things work, but I cannot unhook myself from it either. I moved away at least in part so I that I *could* leave the house in workout clothes without worrying that I would run into someone I know, who would then recount the experience to a mutual acquaintance, "It's a shame, she's really let herself go. Her poor mother!" But I still enjoy playing the game when I'm in town: out to lunch in pressed black cotton shorts, patent leather sandals, a silk blouse. Earrings. Lipstick. Ladies who lunch.

Here is the thing that people (and by people I mean Yankees) often do not get: yes, there are some of us who are faking it, who will turn around and stab you in the back after smiling at you sweetly from ear to ear, who could not care less about the family we've just enquired after, who participate only in the smallest of talk. But the convention and ritual of dress and behavior, proper codes of conduct and decorum, are not simply a cover for wholesale bitchiness. We hold onto all of this in part because it's tradition, but also because we think it makes life better. Baking a casserole when someone dies. Opening the door for a lady, or offering her your seat, or paying for the tab of the young man in fatigues at the airport bar. Saying "Y'all come back now, you hear?" and meaning it. Smiling at babies and striking up conversation with lonely-looking strangers. For most of us, there isn't some complex ulterior motive. It's just what we do.

I attended the twins' baptism, dressed up for church in Ann Taylor-approved attire, posing for pictures afterward with my boys at the front of the church, their sweet heads popping out from all of that fabric like ghosts. From the side of my ear, I could hear Kate's mother explain to puzzled onlookers just who I was and why I was there (because, of course, I was the only brown person in sight). After the service, we all made our way to Kate's parents' grand and stately house for brunch.

Once inside, I headed straight for the master bedroom to stash my coat and purse with the others. Kate stood over the newly baptized, who were smiling and wiggling on the bed. A pile of pastel-colored gift bags mushroomed up from one of the straight-backed chairs in the corner—monogrammed silver things, most likely.

Perhaps it should be noted here that among the first presents John and Henry received was a package of printed calling cards, with their full names and a sweet watercolor picture of a green-and-blue train.

"You know, I'm so relieved," Kate said when she showed them to me, tilting her head to the side a little to indicate sarcasm. "I thought we had gotten all of the essentials, but we didn't even *think* about what the boys would do if they needed to give someone a present."

"Could have been a disastrous start to their social careers," I added solemnly.

It is customary, at least where I am from, for children to have their own calling cards made for the purpose of taping to birthday presents, so as to make the task of keeping up with "who-gave-what-to-whom" much easier. Calling cards are not like junior business cards; they contain only a name, and perhaps some decoration. I still have extra cards leftover from my childhood, stenciled with pretty pink ballet slippers and flowers. Adults utilize more austere versions (ivory cardstock and embossed black ink) to attach their giver-status to casseroles, lasagnas, and other items gifted upon, say, the parents of newborn twins. I didn't realize that not everyone did this until I moved away from Memphis.

After we changed the boys out of their dresses and into much less fussy attire, I walked into the dining room, holding Henry, to check out the spread. Stephen and I had tried to predict the offerings, basing our guesses on the dozens of other receptions, teas, brunches, open houses, and fêtes that come standard with Southern life. Cheese biscuits, fresh fruit, mini-quiche, bite-sized brownies and lemon squares, vegetable crudités and dip, and Parker house rolls with ham and spicy mustard. Most importantly, between the dining room and the kitchen, a short hallway lined on one side by a counter served that morning as the bar.

Since I was holding one of the day's guests of honor, I immediately received a great deal of attention from people I had never before met. Lots of women, cooing and clucking and planting kisses. Henry, already overextended from the day began to squall a bit in my arms. I turned him and shushed him, the usual tricks, while one of the white-haired ladies leaned in to say, "Oh, he says he's upset because doesn't know your face! He doesn't like this strange face! He says he wants his mama! Dear—" she was addressing me now, "You'd better take him to his mother, hmm?"

Stephen jumped in, with an edge to his voice so slight that only someone who knew him well could have detected it. "Oh, he's quite used to that face. Believe me, Nishta knows what she's doing." He gave me a conspiratorial smile and I blushed a little. We had our fair share of instances of my being mistaken for the nanny (brown girl + white dad & white babies = obviously) and plenty of trouble trying to explain exactly what my relationship to the twins *is*. Kate and Stephen have always insisted that I am family, though I'm far from related to the boys by blood. But when you've woken up at two in the morning to give someone a bottle, it induces a sort of claim.

But it would have been impolite to say all of that at a civilized Sunday baptism brunch, so I handed Henry off to his father while David, one of the *official* godparents, walked over from the bar. "Can I get you a drink?" he asked.

"Yes, please," I said. "Bloody Mary?"

"Ah, I didn't take you for a fruity drink kind of girl." A compliment in my book.

David returned with a celery-garnished highball glass, and my first sip was an eye-raiser. "Well, David, this is quite a serious cocktail you've made here."

"You see, this way, you only have to drink the one," he said. "And nobody gets suspicious."

"You've been through one or two of these things before, I take it?"

"Godbless Anglicans who aren't afraid to drink on a Sunday morning," he said, and we clinked glasses.

To visit Memphis today is to experience an almost endless episode of déjà-vu, each place I go stirring up nostalgia, while at the same time adding to it, building the very memories that bind me to this place. It is as if I can see past incarnations of myself everywhere I go, killing time in bookstores and coffee shops, stealing daffodils out of rambling yards, combing the import stores on Summer Avenue for fake Kate Spade purses I could then never bring myself to actually buy, waiting for and then delighting in the autumnal color change of one particularly satisfying oak tree on the corner a few blocks from school, and many, many occasions of being driven: to piano lessons in the dark when the time had changed, to nurseries on the outskirts of the city where I learned to identify "lantana" and "coleus," to Bojangles on Saturday mornings for biscuits, which I took with lots and lots of frighteningly sweet grape jelly.

Perhaps it's the gravitas that comes with having lost a parent in the same place one was born, or the significance imbued by living in one place for eighteen years straight, but Memphis is not just a city to me anymore. The topography, the storefronts, the very street signs have built another kind of map, my very own version of "This Is Your Life." What I drive past, what I miss: the potato soup at Huey's, where the ceiling is littered with fringed toothpicks; the noise at the Rendezvous on Friday nights, with its cold pitchers of beer and shabby plates piled high with dry ribs; $1.10 worth of shaved ice from Jerry's ice cream stand, where the prices haven't changed since they opened in 1979. It never ceases to amaze me how I can feel so safe here and so completely trapped at the same time.

Memphis is changing, and in ways I never dared to hope it could: opening, stretching, revitalizing. I am so proud of, so delighted and often amused by this place, and yet, I cannot imagine myself living here; I never could. I like to think that Memphis always knew it would not win me. And that I can love it now precisely because I'll never live there again.

Our hometowns hold us in a vise grip, a kind of Chinese finger-trap; the more we struggle away from them, the tighter their pull. The Mississippi River and all of its genteel trappings keep me beholden, despite a young lifetime's worth of squirming and scraping against them. Call me on the phone now, and hear me drawl; come over, and I will smile pretty, tie on an apron and bake you up some fine buttermilk biscuits, even if you insist you aren't hungry; I probably won't let you help with the dishes; I'll call you "sir" or "ma'm" regardless of how old you are.

It takes a while to claim what is ours, to allow ourselves to be claimed by it; My name is Nishta, and I am from Memphis.

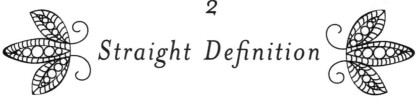

2
Straight Definition

straight (adj.) 3h : heterosexual

For a long time, I thought I was a straight girl: straight ahead, straightforward, straight As, straight answer, straight-laced, get your facts straight. My small and tightly-knit group of friends in late middle school and high school was a mixed-grade motley crew who found each other because each of us didn't really fit in with the rest of the girls in our own respective grades. We were smart in uncommon ways, each a bit too mature and ready to defy conventional habit and stereotypes, which, at an all-girls' Episcopal school in Memphis, meant you didn't have to do anything too extreme; ours was a mild rebellion. We were reverse-snobs, listening to Ani DiFranco, going to see plays instead of going to parties, discussing politics and religion, reading Nietzsche and Simone de Beauvior, writing in journals, and generally fancying ourselves a bad-ass bunch. Though we occupied a small corner of the world at school, we were generally treated well there, finding sympathetic teachers and bemused classmates. And even if our own estimation of our "alternativeness" was inflated, we did live at least a little bit ahead of the curve.

Like any self-respecting group of teenage girls, we had our fair share of drama in the hilariously self-titled "Grrl Gang." Two of our members dated each other, on-again-and-off-again, for years; the nature of the romance was intensified by the logistics of secret-keeping from parents, classmates, and the school. We were a queer group overall—"queer" as the word is used now, a reclamation of what lies outside the norm—with some girls-kissing-girls thrown in for good measure. But even though several of my closest friends weren't straight, and I had no problem with that, I still thought that *I* was. We all did. Especially my parents.

To be fair, I was and still am attracted to men; I didn't fake that. As a teenager, I liked a lot of boys, had crushes on many, mainly older men, which were never reciprocated. Of course, I had had "crushes" on women, too—but the parameters of female friendship, especially at my all-girls' school, left plenty of room for general-ized affection and love. I didn't think of any of it as romantic or out of the ordinary, because it wasn't, explicitly. Then I fell in love with Kassandra.

When I was seventeen, a very close friend and grrl-gang member broke it off with a long-distance girlfriend (whom I really liked) and started dating a brash, cocky, self-proclaimed "artist" named Kassandra, pronounced with a long "a," whom I found at first to be insufferably pretentious. In fact, I could not stand anything about Kassandra when we first met, though she flirted with me shame-lessly and somewhere deep down I couldn't help but be drawn to her swagger. It was when we were all watching a movie, and a preview featuring Jodie Foster came on that I said, without thinking, "She's so hot." Kassandra looked at me sideways and said, "Are you *sure* you're straight?" Then she set about finding out for herself.

Despite my initial dislike and the fact that she was supposed to be dating my friend, Kassandra managed to charm me. We did a lot of talking on the phone and mix-tape exchanging before I made the connection in my brain that I was physically attracted to her. It simply had never occurred to me as a possibility that I might like girls, too, but it sure did explain a heck of a lot when I finally let her kiss me, my first kiss in my very first car, a bright blue Saturn with an open moon roof.

I'll never forget driving home that night, my brain about to explode from all of the contradictory thoughts and worries. I was scared, and I didn't know whom to tell; suddenly, it was clear that I would be in a different category now, according to society, and that my life wasn't going to look the way I had always thought. My parents and classmates were socially liberal, but I didn't know how far their tolerance would extend when it came to me. On some level, it was hilarious, because wasn't I supposed to be the straight girl? The compassionate ally? The one who "got it" but wasn't *in* it?

Of course, I had just had my first kiss, and a good one at that, so the excitement (for whatever came next) and relief (that I was no longer the only "never been kissed" one in my group of friends) that came along with it did a fair job of battling with the doubts, fear, and guilt. In the end, I couldn't deny the reality of what I was feeling; I didn't want to. My whole body rang with the newness of it all. I felt found, and lost, at the same time.

straight (adj.) 1a: free from curves, bends, angles, or irregularities <straight hair>

I styled my hair short for many years, starting my sophomore year of high school, in an attempt to look older and more sophisticated. It ranged from ear-length to pixie-short, and though I never consciously connected my hair to my sexuality, I know others did. Conscious or not, it was code—*I'm not like the other girls, and I don't want to be*—and my father read that code clearly and fought against it. He long harbored visions of me with flowing tresses like the hip-shaking heroines of the Bollywood movies he loved to watch. And so it became the running family joke; my bald father would tell me to "Grow it out!" and "Don't get it cut so short this time!" and I would tell him, "If you want long hair, then grow it yourself."

My father started losing his hair when he was in his early twenties. One of my favorite pictures of him is from the time before he went bald, a version of him I never knew. The photograph is black-and-white; my father wears a suit and sunglasses, his hands in his pockets, handsome and stoic. On his head, more hair than I ever saw him with my whole life: medium-thick in soft waves, lustrous and dark, just like mine.

I grew up in a family of three: Subhash, Veena, Nishta. Three is a tricky number to navigate. Three people equals four relationships.

Subhash and Veena. Subhash and Nishta. Veena and Nishta. Subhash, Veena, and Nishta. My mother was fully a mother, fully desirous of being so, having tried so hard and for so long and with so much sadness tied up in it. I know that my father was equally excited to have a child, didn't fake his enthusiasm for parenthood or do it because my mother wanted him to, but still, it meant something different to him than it did to her. My mother's attention toward me was inexhaustible. Being my mother was the whole of her identity; all other functions, obligations, and responsibilities were, to varying degrees, tangential. Not that she indulged me—she was firm and strict where my father was inclined to spoil—rather, she indulged herself. I may have been my father's darling, but I was one-hundred-percent my mother's child, and it was primarily through her cues that I developed my relationship with him.

I think that the power of his wife's insistent mothering left my father with little room to squeeze in between her and me. Though I didn't see it at the time, I was often my mother's conspirator when discontent or argument got the better of my parents. I would watch them from the carpeted staircase, which went up eight steps to a landing then flipped around and went upward for another eight. A picture frame, three feet by two feet, full of little circles, rectangles, and squares, in which happy scenes of my young parents and baby self peeked out, hung at the top of the first flight of stairs. Hidden behind the wall which separated the top stairs from the bottom ones, I could see the lights and figures in the kitchen reflected on the glass, and hear easily every word, until I got older and they got wise and started closing the kitchen doors.

These arguments would come to a head, my mother charging upstairs to my parents' bedroom, my father remaining downstairs for some solitude. After enough time had passed, I would slide quietly, softly into my parents' bedroom and into my mother's lap. I felt it was my job to make her feel better, to let her air her grievances and then pad downstairs to see my father, whose face and tone betrayed only that he was tired. As we all grew older, *I* became the center of the arguments, and of course I fought back. We, the women in my father's life, slamming our way through his house as he did his best either to play mediator or stay quiet. I started to lean into him then, realizing that he had fifteen years on me when it came to my mother. He would explain to me about her, how I could be more diplomatic, that I shouldn't provoke her, that she didn't mean to say those things. I began to see him more, see him differently in those times.

straight (adj.) 3a : exhibiting honesty and fairness <straight dealing>
b : properly ordered or arranged

When I started dating Kassandra, my mom thought I was doing drugs. My father was completely clueless. I never could—still can't—lie to my mother, and so, when she confronted me, I told her the truth, which I thought would surely come as a relief. What's kissing a girl to smoking pot? As it turns out, I think my mother would have found pot smoking to be preferable, because at least it was within the realm of possibility of her planning, things she had considered, things she felt she could deal with. My mother is a woman who obsessively makes lists, who will walk across the room to flick a light switch so the ones on the other side of the room will stay lined up, all facing up or all facing down. More than any cultural disapproval or moral confusion, I believe what bothered my mom most about my dating a girl was that she hadn't seen it coming. She had never prepared for the possibility that her little girl would not grow up to fall in love and marry a man (even a white man! my parents were so prepared to give me that one), have babies, and so on.

She kept my relationship with Kassandra a secret from my father for a few months, assured in her mind that it was simply a "phase" I would grow out of, one of the dangers of raising your children in America, where they get all kinds of strange notions in their heads. Then, during a family argument, my mother outed me to my father as a kind of punishment for him taking my side. "You think she's so blameless? You want to know what's she's doing, what she's keeping from you?" Initially, he was angry, shocked, and disappointed. Then he decided he would talk me out of being gay.

Talking was his way; yelling was my Mom's. Dad liked to "cap-ital-T" Talk in the living room, the most expensively decorated room in the house, and therefore the least used. My Yamaha piano upright in one corner, a glass curio cabinet in another, rugs from India stretched across the floor, and crown molding & a gold border edging the ceiling like icing. My father's favorite chair, a boxy but comfortable thing upholstered in silver-blue fabric, sat up against the window in front of lacy curtains and with a view of the street, partially blocked by the greenery of my mother's meticulously tended front yard.

The living room and its chair served as the backdrop for all things serious and important—every picture ever taken of me dressed up for a special occasion (piano recital, wedding, graduation) was taken in that room, with me either in the chair or next to it, piano visible off to one side. It was in the living room that my father congratulated me on getting my first period, telling me "You're a woman now, I'm very proud of you," me sitting on one arm of the chair, half pleased, half totally mortified. This is where my father would read the paper on weekend mornings, and where he'd ask if he could sit and listen while I practiced piano.

"Nito, please come into the living room," always meant that I was in for something. No matter how congenial he looked in his chair, I knew that a "discussion," by which he usually meant lecture, was about to take place. But the difference in our conversation about my sexuality was that I could not see that I had done anything wrong. I didn't feel that I had anything to apologize for, other than keeping a secret from him. I was happy, but that didn't seem to matter. My father saw my relationship with Kassandra as a choice, one that I could only be making spitefully, to hurt him and to dishonor every-thing my parents had ever done for me. How difficult it would be for them, and how embarrassing.

After that conversation, and my inability to respond in any way other than insulted and pissed off, my father stopped speaking to me for about three months. He said things like "Pass the salt" and "Goodnight," and acted perfectly normal towards me in public, but for most of the second semester of my senior year of high school, he and I were frozen in silence.

straight (adj.) 2a : lying along or holding to a direct or proper course or method <a straight thinker> b : candid, frank <a straight answer>

I buzzed all of my hair off my freshman year of college, the result of a social experiment that I undertook with my fortuitously-assigned roommate Rebecca. She was from a small town just outside of Ft. Worth, Texas, the youngest of three siblings, and the product of a Santayana-reading Mexican father and a sweet-and-naïve-as-pie, Church of Christ-adherent mother. In her efforts to mix these two parts of herself, Rebecca was, at nineteen, bolder and more defiant than I could conceive of being. She was my first true friend on campus, and shaving our heads was her idea.

You can guess how two girls with shaved heads who go everywhere together and do everything together are seen, but the funny thing is that while you could have connected *my* lack of hair to my sexuality, Rebecca is the straightest girl I know. To the stereotyping eye, she's often mistaken for a lesbian; we have long joked that she would make a better one than me. She rarely wears skirts, knows how to repair all kinds things, has worked construction, lusts after motorcycles, and doesn't like spending money on shoes or makeup. I, on the other hand, am a preppy, J. Crew-buying, high-heel-wearing, mechanically-indifferent lipstick lesbian.

When we met, Rebecca was already practiced at rebellion, busy untangling herself from her mother's world inch by inch. But even though I was scandalously "out," I was still deeply attached to what people thought, trying to square the ideal of the proper Southern world I was brought up in with the new things I had discovered about myself and the world at large. Given all of that, there seemed no more direct or immediate way for me to force myself to deal with who I was and who I wanted to be than to shave my head; at the very least, I figured "Why the hell not?"

Everyone else assumed I was having some kind of angry lesbian moment, but I wasn't really all that angry. I shaved my head because I *could*. I was in college, away from home for the first time and drunk on that exhilarating sense of utter freedom and rapacious, but simultaneously innocent, self-involvement. I didn't have to find a job. I didn't owe anyone anything, in my estimation. More than anything, I wanted to know if I *could* do it. If I could be the kind of person who shaves her head for no good reason. If I could stand the looks and snickers and detach myself from my appearance enough to practice not giving a shit what other people thought. There was a healthy dose of daredevil, too, but overall it was an earnest undertaking. *It's just hair,* I thought.

To my surprise and perhaps disappointment, my father handled my shaved head remarkably well, voicing no critiques and even silencing my mother who clearly thought I had lost my mind. He and I had reconnected to a certain extent, as a result of the distance, and no doubt, too, as a result of the boyfriend I had for a few months during my first semester of college. But I never straight-out asked my father what he thought of my shorn head; I think I was probably afraid to hear how he really felt. Perhaps a shaved head was too far beyond anything he felt he could joke about; perhaps it felt like a slap in the face, a deliberate separation from everything he had wanted for me, and from me.

In college, my relationship with my parents healed, then tore again, like a scab that kept crusting over. We maintained our own kind of "Don't Ask, Don't Tell" policy until I could no longer bear it, longing for the closeness that once had been. I had to come out to them a second time, sort of an "I'm a lesbian for real" phone conversation that I remember little of; it was so awful that I trained myself to put it out of my mind. My father followed up with a many-page, handwritten letter, so wounded and manipulative in content that I completely blocked the memory of it, too, rediscovering it only after his death, when I found among his papers a copy of the letter that he had made for himself to keep. For my part, I was in my early twenties and more entitled than compassionate with my wounded parents, unable to fathom how my self-expression could break their hearts.

Lest it sound like I had some terrible kind of family life, it's important to know that I never stopped loving my parents or feeling loved by them. I still enjoyed seeing and spending time with them; I missed them. I would never have spoken ill of them to anyone. It's difficult to separate what would have naturally occurred as part of the leaving-home-and-differentiating-your-identity growing pains from the intensity that my sexuality brought to the table. Frustrated and disappointed in them though I was, I remained grateful to them and defensive of them. And the perspective that came with being away from home and broadening my world allowed me to cut them some slack, realize how lucky I was. For their part, my parents never stopped paying my way, never even threatened to, and they continued to encourage me academically, telling me they were proud of the things they were proud of.

But we were split—a whole side of my life I didn't speak about, including the serious relationship I had begun with Jill—and a whole glacier's worth of worry and disappointment on their side that I only caught a glimpse of from time to time. I heard accounts of it from my mother, which continued the pattern of splitting our family, unfairly weighing the relationships contained within.

"He never even talks about you! He doesn't even mention your name anymore, it's like you don't exist." When he did speak about me, I gathered, it was with anger, the cloak of the betrayed, since he believed that I had selfishly chosen a life that would humiliate and disappoint my parents, my parents who worked so hard their whole lives to give me everything I ever wanted.

straight (adj.) g (1) : exhibiting no deviation from what is established or accepted as usual, normal, or proper : conventional

Though I never shaved it again, I continued to style my hair short. Then, in my first semester of graduate school, my parents proposed a trip to India for my cousin's wedding. She was three years my junior and had become engaged to a man that she had met at another family wedding and secretly "dated" before coming home and suggesting to her parents that he might be a good match for her. I rather liked this scheme; it was spunky and made the prospect of braving a wedding (at which I would be the noticeably older, unmarried, American cousin) far more palatable. Not to mention, I had not been to India, the country of my parents' birth, in over a decade, and my father and I had only traveled there together once before, when I was an infant.

The idea of India began to glow in my mind with increasing intensity, the way we often fall in love with ideas without knowing much at all about what they represent. What such a trip might mean I could barely articulate, but it lived in my imagination like a warm, luminous piece of fruit, many-layered and ripe for the picking. The timing seemed just right, as I was in graduate school (getting a writing degree, no less), prone to introspection, accustomed to watching closely and taking notes. I had also, at long last, reached a certain plane of adulthood that allowed me to become more generous with my parents; they, in turn, were beginning to relax a little as they started to accept that I was turning out to be the responsible, self-sufficient adult they had worked so hard to raise and that my sexuality wasn't, apparently, ruining my life.

All of these factors knit together, allowing me to understand just how much there was for me to understand—my parents, my extended family, my second language, my connection to a country at once both intimate and exotic. I was determined to take our trip to India seriously. I practiced my Hindi and got an ungodly number of shots, my parents busy booking flights and planning an elaborate itinerary of which relatives we would be staying with, and when. We were scheduled to be in India for a total of three weeks.

That Thanksgiving, my parents came to visit me in Tucson, where I was attending graduate school. They discovered that their daughter was a grownup who could cook them a lovely dinner, chauffeur them around town, do the dishes, mix them a gin and tonic. There was something new about that visit, not merely its location. I introduced my parents to my new friends, a big pack of artsy lesbians who were very lovely and generous with them, and what do you know? My parents were lovely and generous back, a little cautious, but no extra commentary, a separate peace, a truce. Of course, we did not speak about Jill; she was, by default, A Secret. And she and I were, by default, by family circumstance and distance, used to not spending the holidays together, in marked contrast to what married couples, or even boyfriend-and-girlfriend couples, mostly do.

In the way that family secrets work, I do not think there was in fact anything *actually* secret about Jill. "Secret" as in "We don't talk about that." Whatever my parents may have suspected, they did not say anything, not even to each other. I was ready to speak about my love life, if asked, but it's nice sometimes to go along with the illusion that everything is working just fine, because here we are, laughing at *The Daily Show,* and here we are, driving down twisty mountain roads with an unfairly beautiful Arizona sunset in the backdrop and here I am, compartmentalizing my life. The three of us, my parents and I, chose the closeness that came with quiet.

A month later, at Christmas, I flew home to visit my parents. My father took me out for a traditional holiday lunch at Corky's, one of the best places to eat pulled pork in Memphis. Through the years, the restaurant had become the ultimate father-daughter spot, typifying everything about the deep, epicurean pleasure that my father valued. The original Corky's building is easy to pick out: plumes of smoke waft up from the pit house, cords of hardwood are stacked around the building, and the parking lot is almost always full. Inside, signed, glossy headshots line the walls of the waiting room, everyone from former Miss Americas to former Presidents and Vice-Presidents. "Trophy" copies of magazine and newspaper articles tell visitors what they should already know; they are about to eat the best of the best.

There we were, my father and I, unabashed meat lovers both, sitting in Corky's darkened dining room and ordering our standard: two unsweet teas with lemon, a basket of rolls, a half-loaf of onion rings, and two pulled pork sandwiches (slaw-on, Memphis style) with a side of baked beans. The restaurant's familiar soundtrack looped from Jerry Lee Lewis to Elvis to Ike and Tina Turner as we dug in.

I have to give him credit, for it was a very clever tactical move on the part of my father, loading me up on barbecue sauce before discussing my hair. My favorite food, coupled with childhood nostalgia? I didn't stand a chance.

"Nito," he said, just as I was settling into my meat coma, "What if you grew your hair for a little while? Please don't cut it before we go to India. It will just look better, your relatives will like to see it, not so short."

I knew that my relatives weren't the only ones who would like to see my hair "not so short," but refrained from saying so. To be fair, I knew that in combination with my un-pierced ears and dark skin, my short hair did make me look to traditional Indian eyes like an utterly shameless rebel.

"But doesn't the nose ring count for anything?" I asked him, mostly teasing since I had pierced it on a whim in college, not out of any deep-seated cultural agenda.

"Maybe a five-point bonus," he said, keeping the joke. "But your hair could look so nice!"

He said "could," as in "doesn't right now," which I noticed but also choose to ignore. Instead, I decided to leave my hair untouched. After all, I had cut it for no particular reason, surely I could grow it out when it meant so much to my father. He rarely made requests of me anymore, ever since I had made it clear I didn't want or need him in my business.

"I'm going to cut it as soon as we get back, though, okay?"

"Okay," he consented. "It's your hair."

The following May, my parents picked me up from the Memphis airport, bubbling with last-minute travel preparations; only two days until we would return to depart for India. They hugged me, asked if I was hungry. I was genuinely happy to see them, breathe in the humid air of my hometown.

"Wow, *shashajee*, your hair is so long," my mother marveled, using one of her dozens of half-Hindi, half-English nicknames for me.

"I know, it's driving me nuts," I said, tugging on a strand as if to demonstrate the obvious bad state of my growing-it-out look.

"I think it looks good," Dad said, "Very nice."

"Yeah, I know *you* like it," I teased him. "It was your idea!"

"And see, I was right. You look so good, like a normal person now."

Like a normal person. Like a straight girl? Like a good, obedient Indian daughter? Is that what he was getting at? The teenager in me wanted to sass, "What's *that* supposed to mean?" But instead, I thought, *Play nice* and sighed, "Sure dad, whatever you say."

> *straight (adj.) d (1) : having the elements in an order <the straight sequence of events>*

My father and I walked past the windowed shops in the Detroit Airport's International Terminal, headed for the large duty-free store at the busy corner ahead. We were on our way to buy cognac, and we were holding hands. I was surprised; it had been a long time. There was a great deal of distance between the way we interacted in my adulthood and the shoulder-rides and easy snuggling of my youth. He had never been one of those reserved, pat-on-the-back kind of Dads, thank goodness. My father was always quick and eager to say "I love you" and to hug me until, well, until he wasn't. Our loss of intimacy was measured, deliberate even.

For so long, I chose to believe that it was *his* job to make our relationship work. But something about the demilitarized zone of airport space allowed me to see that I hadn't been giving him much to work with. Gratefully I found that the shape of my father's hand felt familiar, warm, flat, dry, and comfortingly bigger than mine. We walked easily, hands loosely clasped and arms swinging gently. I slowed my pace to match my father's and set to window-shopping, people-watching. Our conversation was idle chatter, travel logistics and the like, in that way which people seem to need to discuss and rehearse whatever it is they are about to experience, but the feeling of walking with him, hand-in-hand, made me think for the first time in a long time that our relationship was on its way back.

As we walked, I noticed a pair of brown faces, part of a family of five which also set up camp at our departure gate. The father, in his thirties, was walking with his youngest daughter, three or four years old, shiny, dark hair cropped into a messy bowl cut. They were holding hands too, though at a more lopsided angle. I nudged my dad in their direction, "Look."

"Little *jungu*," he said, smiling. *Jungu* is a Punjabi colloquialism that means something like "doofus," although my father, over many years, managed to transform it into a term of affection and used it almost exclusively in reference to me.

"I'll bet they're not on their way to buy alcohol," I grinned. The cognac was being purchased as a gift for the family branch that was hosting us in Mumbai.

"No," he laughed. "Probably not. Probably candy."

"Chocolate," I guessed.

Our hands dropped as we round the corner and crossed into the duty-free shop. But we held them again on our way back to meet my mom at the gate. A few seats over, the little *jungu* returned with her father, he holding a bag from McDonald's, she with a French fry already in her mouth.

straight (adj.) 1b : generated by a point moving continuously in the same direction and expressed by a linear equation <a straight line>

My father had an incredible mind for numbers, real skill and passion and a facility for helping others understand them, too. Throughout middle and high school I largely eschewed his help, in an inverse relationship to how much I needed it. His desire for me to do well in his favorite subject felt, to my stubborn and willful self, too connected to him. I didn't do poorly on purpose (and I didn't do all that poorly, all things considered, but you've probably heard that a "B" is an "Asian F"), but I didn't seek out his help, either.

Then I took AP Calculus my senior year of high school; at the semester break, I had my first and only C+, the existence of which I wound up sharing with a reporter from U.S. News and World Report in a story about college admissions. The story detailed my choice to stay in the class instead of dropping down to something easier, despite the risk that the grade would be a red flag for colleges. My father and I argued over this very set of options over the phone that December, me assuring him that my Calculus teacher felt I should stick it out, him heartsick that his child had done so poorly in a subject he loved so much. I wound up pulling up my grade, getting into college, and earning a 4 on the AP Calculus exam. In the scrapbooks she made for me after I left home, my mother has clipped the *US News & World Report* article and pasted it onto a page with the caption, "Now the whole world knows I made a C!"

When I was a senior in college and applying to graduate school, I bought a book to help me prepare for the math section of the GRE. Even though I was going to school to earn an MFA in Creative Writing, I still didn't want to embarrass myself with a dismal math score. It had been four years since I had done math of any kind, and in that time I had become a reasonable enough human being to actually consider asking my dad for help. I drove home for a long weekend in October.

As it turned out, he was a marvelous teacher: patient and encouraging, experienced from the volunteer SAT tutoring he had taken up after I left home (in which he found a more grateful audience than I had ever been). He and I worked hard, practicing problems on the yellow legal pad, his sloping handwriting so distinctive, the sight of him correcting my mistakes no longer making me as resentful as it once had. My mom brought tea and snacks to the kitchen table while we plowed through sample problems for three days. I took the GRE, acing the verbal section and earning a very respectable score in math.

straight (adj.) 3c : free from extraneous matter : unmixed <straight whiskey> d : marked by no exceptions or deviations in support of a principle

We didn't end up going to my cousin's wedding. Her father-in-law-to-be was killed in a car accident just a few weeks before our trip, and so the celebration was pushed back six months to allow a proper period of mourning. For my parents and I to reschedule our trip, though, would have meant considerable logistical and financial wrangling—not to mention the improbability that the three of us would have been able to line up three weeks of time together again.

"I wish you could have seen a *real* Indian wedding," my mom sighed. "A real-life *Monsoon Wedding*." I, too, wanted add another authentic cultural event to my experience, instead of knowing these things only through movies or the transplanted American versions. But a huge part of me felt relieved, the part that was terrified by the prospect of being surrounded by hundreds of strangers who somehow had a claim over me, would want to hug me and talk to me and inquire of my mother when my *shaddhi* would be, when they could look forward to standing around and doing this at *my* wedding. My poor mother, who absolutely abhors small talk and is terrible at faking things, who is sad enough on her own that there isn't going to be a *shaddhi* for her baby girl, was spared at least that one thing.

At some point during our trip, the gravity hit me; it's a big deal that I'm not getting married. Not that anyone said so directly (the only people who knew, of course, about my inevitable "unmarried" status were my parents), but with every day that went by, I heard at least one conversation about weddings and marriage, a discussion about the details and plans and arrangements, reminiscence over so-and-so's nuptials, worry over finding a good match for a son or daughter, and fretting about the increasingly prevalent trend of dating and premarital sex. *Shaddhi, shaddhi, shaddhi.* It's like that's all they could talk about. Of course, this isn't too terribly different from Memphis, from lipsticked old biddies who smile at you knowingly and say, "Are you seeing anybody *special*, dear?" But at least there I could answer "Yes, and she's just wonderful," and make my point clear, even if I did cause a scandal. In India, there is no language other than heterosexual. And way more so than Hindi, I felt expected to speak it.

On a flight from Delhi to Mumbai, I found myself being flirted with by a terribly handsome, turbaned flight attendant; or rather, flirted with to whatever extent any young man can flirt with a young woman who is sitting next to her parents, in India or elsewhere. I was happy to give him a shy smile with my "thank you," and wasn't above applying lip gloss in the bathroom for his benefit; I may be a lesbian but I'm also an incorrigible flirt. But something deeper and more complicated pulled at me, thousands of miles away from my "other" life in America. It almost didn't seem possible that I *had* an other life, so intense was the world I found myself in at the time. This flight attendant, perfectly harmless in his uniform and with his Continental accent, felt like flash of an alternative life, sent deliberately to test me and see if I wouldn't just give in to the life I knew my parents would prefer for me: white-picket fence, brown husband, brown children, the whole shebang. For about fifteen minutes, it seemed that it would all be simpler; I could have my intimacy with my parents back, and there would be no more letters, no more awkward phone calls, no more arguments about the "choice" I was making. Had I not already been in love with and committed to Jill at the time, I think I would have wrestled with it longer. Asian daughter's duty versus American daughter's personal happiness—what is the right choice when you are hyphenated between?

My father fell asleep on the plane, and he began snoring on my shoulder halfway during our flight, which made my Mom giggle and made me really glad. With our closeness ratcheting up day by day, I wondered if we just might make it back home in a whole new light.

straight (adj.) 2d (1) : having the elements in an order <the straight sequence of events>

My father died six weeks after we returned from India: an interstitial lung disease that came out of the blue and kept him in the hospital for just under three weeks, unresponsive to any treatment. I was at his bedside for most of that time, devastated but grateful that the new dynamic we had worked to forge in India seemed to have transferred back home, for however brief a period.

Since saying goodbye to him on July 22 of 2006, I have kept my hair long with just three exceptions: donations to an organization that provides wigs at low cost to women who go bald while fighting cancer, part of a promise made to my college roommate Rebecca's mom, who died just months after my father. Ironic, since in most cultures, hair is shorn or even shaved when mourning—but that, of course, would have been the last thing my dad would want.

When someone dies, you begin to think about the project of wrapping up their life, your lives together, gliding an index finger down a ledger of accounts, taking inventory, making a reckoning. I want to know how the math works; I need him to help me balance the equation of our time together. Does this one thing cancel out everything else? How does it add up, Papa? Teach me, I can't figure it out.

3

Amritsar

And so I tell my life to myself.
-Frederich Nietzsche

Perhaps it is a generational symptom, or hazard, to experience times in one's life that are later identified as having felt "like a movie." If serendipity, luck, or chance has played a large part, making our day close to perfect or delightfully surprising, then "it was like a movie." If terrible things have taken place, things no one could have foreseen, things we feel we might not make it through, then "it was like a movie," also. We play a soundtrack in our minds, imagine the cinematography, frame the camera angles. This makes us sound narcissistic, which is true—another generational hazard—but it is also true that humans have long been engaged with the project of narrating their own lives: making sense, making meaning. Then it was cave painting, now it is film; life informs art, and vice-versa.

Nearly everything about the summer of 2006 occurs in my remembering like a movie. All of it is showcased, projected up on the screen of my mind as if it happened to someone else. As if it had been written, with a tidy narrative arc, complete alignment of feeling and form, shot on location in India, the last major motion picture in which my father would ever appear.

Subhash Chander Mehra was born on April twenty-seventh, 1942. He was the middle child, preceded by two sisters and followed by two brothers. Santoj, Sudarshan, Subhash, Sudesh, and Sharath. I think it's adorable, the way their names fall into line like that. I don't have any access to the sibling experience, but I know my father's place in the family line informed nearly every action of his life. As a first-born male in India, he made a natural protagonist, doted upon by his sisters, idolized by his younger brothers. But that's the language of this place, this world: my context, my tongue. The vocabulary of the world I'm sitting in today bears little or no relation to the cramped alleyways in which my father grew up. And it's when we are lazy with our thinking that things become lost in translation.

His family was poor—not destitute, but crowded into a cluster of third-story, third-world rooms—a laundry-hanging, paint-chipping, stinking kind of place with exposed wires and pipes and rickety staircases that I had before only imagined or seen in, of course, movies. Then suddenly I was standing in the room where my father was born. It seems absurd and sad to me now that during our time in his hometown, Amritsar, I followed my father, camera in hand, conceiving and carrying myself as if I were making a documentary, the thoughtful Western journalist exploring an exotic place, yet again needing fiction with which to frame reality.

Now, from my position of hindsight, I pause the screen of my memory and count forward in weeks. Was it happening then, right in front of me? My father's lungs quickly building honeycomb, the fibrotic tissue that would kill him just weeks later, as he showed me the rooms he remembered, the one bathroom they shared with two other families, the second-story railing where two-year-old Sudesh fell and hit his head, rendering him what they called "slow" for the rest of his life. And there I was, twenty-three years old, dressed in the same, colorful clothing as everyone else, but much too tall for a girl, with hair much too short, my sunglasses and my bag undeniably new. My ears not pierced, though my nose was. American—used to walking on sidewalks, to well-ordered lanes of traffic, to all kinds of signifiers that remain transparent until we step on someone else's soil. My father's soil.

Amritsar was the only place I traveled to in India where I felt like a real novelty. On the street, a young girl walked up to me and wanted to shake my hand, asked me what my name was and if I were from America. *Mera nam Nishta hai*, the first day of Hindi 101 thankfully coming back to me. *Hanji, America.*

There are only so many stories to be told, when you get down to skin and bone and human relationship. Our details differ, but there is a reason that the same tales keep getting replayed over and over again: we are slow to learn. As supposedly self-aware as I was, it took my breathing the air on the complete other side of the world for me to see my father's life for what it was. How could I not have seen it before? How could my story turn out so cliché? I didn't even know the half of it.

Flying to India usually requires flying to somewhere in Europe first—in my family's case, in May of 2006, that "somewhere" was Amsterdam. On the plane, our assigned seats were split, so I offered to settle into the seat a few rows ahead of my parents, grabbing what I knew would be one of the last opportunities for privacy on the trip. I began to get the feeling that I was totally unprepared for what lay ahead. I should have asked more questions—what exactly were we going to *do* for three weeks in India? What was I supposed to *say* to my relatives, whom I had not seen in twelve years? Was it even *possible* to know them, to get to know them, for them to get to know me? What if the contexts were too radically different?

As a kid, I remember my parents connecting emotionally, lovingly with voices on the other end of a telephone line that often blanket: cooing words and sometimes crying into the phone, missing a world I did not know. For years, I did my best to hide or fake being tired or sick, sometimes even begging to avoid having to hold the phone up to my own ear, speak to people who were my family by definition only: "Please don't make me talk!" *I don't know who those people are.*

After long naps in the Amsterdam airport, my parents and I flew into Mumbai, this time seated together, my father and I near the window, my mother across the aisle from us. I had a geeky doorstop of a book for reading, Peter Brown's definitive biography of Augustine, but my cruising altitude brain could only seem to handle small, simple chunks of information. Air travel compresses time in such a way that the brain doesn't really have the chance to process what's going on—I am leaving one place for another; I am traveling between worlds. My trip to India marked the halfway point of two years' worth of a long-distance relationship with my partner Jill, in which one of us would fly twelve hundred miles every four-to-six weeks to see the other. I remember being frustrated with the deftness with which I could be airlifted from one reality to another: leg thrown around my love in the morning, but eating a solo dinner later that night. Never enough time to identify and articulate what was happening, or about to happen, or had already happened.

The same held true on this trip. Once our in-flight movie had run its course, the screen filled with a map, a graphic of our plane's route from Amsterdam to Mumbai, with a time-delayed representation of where we were, now and now and now. Out of the corner of my eye, I watched the honeybee inch its way across waters towards the Indian peninsula as my parents charted the family tree for me, solidifying my sense of who was married to whom, who was on good terms with whom, and the proper titles by which they should all be addressed. "When in doubt, just call someone 'uncle' or 'aunty'—you can't go wrong," my father said with a joking smile.

"I'm nervous," I confessed. He reached over, grabbed my hand again, and kissed the back of it. What I didn't say was that I was almost just as nervous to be spending three weeks with *him* as I was the practical strangers that made up my extended family. So far things had been good, but I was busy waiting for the other shoe to drop, as was my habit, as if all of this good feeling and connectedness were suddenly going to be canceled out when my father remembered how much I had disappointed him by "choosing" to be a lesbian. It's like he loved me in spite of himself; he wanted to be mad at me, but now that we were face-to-face, he couldn't pull it off. And I couldn't either. Of course my mind kept racing ahead, refusing to stay present, flitting in and out of future conversations, to the likely fact that my father was never going to approve of my life, never happily hug Jill, never be excited to come to Thanksgiving dinner at our house. And I didn't know what to do about it.

Outside the window, dark sky gave way to a whole city on the water. For the first time since we left Memphis, I had the distinct feeling that we were *somewhere else*, a whole world which I did not know but in which my parents came to be. I looked over at my father and saw tears in his eyes. His emotion jolted me, an ego check. All of my talk and excitement about the trip had centered around what it would offer *me*, a chance to connect with some part of myself that I did not know, to see beautiful things and eat amazing food and mine it all for writing material. Even my conception of what it meant to be traveling with my parents revolved around me—*my* nerves, *my* wondering, *my* discomfort, *my* hope. But the fact that there was an entirely separate side to these people, my parents, that this trip might mean things to them which had nothing to do with me—it was a thought I had somehow, up to that point, not entertained.

This was the land of their birth, the place where all of their blood relatives (except me) lived. This is the culture they knew first, the mother tongue, the place where they were not immigrants but expats. India was the seat of their memory, their childhoods, their mothers (both of whom my parents lost young). India was family dynamics and logistics, was not having to feel self-conscious eating with your hands, was showing off their American daughter and wondering if they had made a mistake in raising her somewhere else.

A cinematic detail: I always thought my parents weren't "nature people" because I grew up without learning the names of any birds or trees. Within fifteen minutes of being on India soil, my mother pointed out two different plants and named their

medicinal and edible qualities. My father identified a bird call
in the distance. All along, I had been looking for field guides on
the wrong continent.

What hit me first as we moved through the Mumbai Airport was
that all of the people were brown. Not just brown, but *my* kind of
brown. I was totally thrown. Only on a college tour of Stanford had
I seen so many brown people in once place before (no joke). I was
so accustomed to being in the minority, color-wise, wherever I went,
that to be able to blend in for once felt strange.

Once we had retrieved our bags from customs and headed outside, I was crushed not only by the humidity but also by a third of
my family tree, as if they had jumped off the pages of my journal
where my parents had just recorded their names and connected
relationships for my benefit. Two in the morning, and still they
were all there, had been waiting for us, for the family to return. I
hugged and kissed and I felt joy, real joy, at this prospect of being
loved without having to earn it—a prospect which had not been so
abundantly available to me since I was born. "Here," they seemed
to be saying, "You belong to us."

My father was clearly the patriarch, eldest brother, kind uncle,
smiling easily at the baby girls, making them duck their chins and
giggle. I began to understand what a special thing we were, the ones
who left, the ones who came back to visit. Before me were huge,
complex matrices of relatedness and history, human desire and story,
all lying just beneath the surface. Humbled, I made myself suddenly
shy and speechless, and felt relieved and overwhelmed when we were
folded into my cousin's car and driven through the gloaming city.

A couple of hours of sleep and a cup of strong, milky tea later,
I stood watching out the window of my family's seventh-floor flat.
There were parrots on the power line, the clown-colored kind that,
in America, you normally see only in zoos, and street dogs running

out on the open field across from the building. Rows and rows of what can only be called hovels lined the streets, their inhabitants going about their morning business in full view as taxis and cars and bicycle rickshaws zoomed by. The pace seemed at once faster and slower than what I was accustomed to. Everything was closer together: the buildings, the people, the traffic. And always the noise: noise from the parrots, noise from the window unit, noise of the honking and barking and arguing and greeting. City noise, the mass of humanity.

Already things felt easy, easier than I ever would have expected. Like an instant transport to another reality, my consciousness soon caught up with my surroundings. I found my mouth forming the words for the proper familial titles, *bhua* for my father's sister, *bhaiya* to refer to my first cousin, Anil, as a brother, and *bhabi* for his wife, Varsha. Their daughters, Meenakshi and Anshu, are my second cousins but close to my age, just three and five years younger. For this reason they call me *didi*, for older sister, instead of *masi*, for aunt. I, the only child, have never been anyone's big sister, and I loved the sound of it. Though it hardly made sense, I found myself filled with the most genuine love and affection for these people.

Things I did not expect: to like the feel of squatting naked for showers on the bathroom floor, pouring half-cold, half-warm water from a bucket over my head. To not mind sleeping on a trundle bed next to my parents with the noise of the world's largest city seeping in through the windows. That everything would taste *so good*. Even more surprisingly: that my parents knew me, they got me, they had been paying attention even though I didn't think they were. Two days into our trip, I even heard my father brag, "My daughter is a real scholar," which shocked me to no end. Here I had been going along thinking that with my B.A. and soon-to-be M.F.A, I had committed the cardinal sin of breaking ranks from that familiar ethnic expectation, from crib to cap-and-gown, "Maybe she will be a doctor, or engineer!" I didn't even do second-best, law or business school, and lived in fear of those "How are you going to make money?" and "What are you going to do with *that*?" conversations that are so standard in our community. But my father sounded proud, genuinely so, on board with the person his daughter had become.

Perhaps it was all context, his happiness at being home, surrounded by family, people around all of time to hear stories and have tea together, the way he liked it, the way he grew up. But it started to be easy for us to be together again, easy in a way that was contagious and almost felt like magic. So I decided to give him a new name. Plain-old American "Dad" didn't work in this new place, and "Daddo," my old standby, was too little-girl, too tied to what we used to have. "Papa" is what I decided on, a little bit American, a little bit Indian, a lot old fashioned, and just right for someone like me who consciously names and differentiates, who trusts the power of words to mark things like new eras and ways of being. The moniker took hold easily; I could tell that he liked it. "Papa, no cheating!" I heard myself chiding one afternoon, ten of us piled onto a giant bed, playing cards.

New scene, from one of our first mornings in Mumbai. Roll tape, action: My father and I go out for a walk, just the two of us, traveling down the rickety elevator of his sister's flat and out into the street. We work our way across a few busy streets to the Five Gardens, where paths are reserved for pedestrians and where I am surprised to see men and women walking with headphones and tennis shoes on, albeit in their *salwar kameezes* and *kurtas*. The gardens are really more like well-shaded parks gated off from traffic. Of course, nearly everywhere you turn in Mumbai is a veritable garden; given the hothouse climate, all manner of flowers and greenery grow.

Each of the five gardens contains a different buzz of activity—a rousing game of cricket underway on one dusty circle, some quiet games of chess between old men under the shade of palm trees. We stop to watch the cricket match and I realize I am more rabidly American than I ever imagined, since I know and love everything about baseball but have no idea how to even follow this game, the game that the British gave to my people and at which we continually out-do them. One of the sharp-edged ironies of colonialism is this: the colonized often long to be like their colonizers. They learn to emulate the imperialists' tastes in dress, accent, mannerism, and drink at the same time that they struggle to be free from them. *We'll take what's yours, only we'll do it one better:* small victories for the conquered. Want to appropriate us? By golly, we'll appropriate you.

My father exhibited this tendency in his own small and bizarre ways, refusing to buy gas from "British Petroleum" and cursing the United Kingdom at every opportunity. At the same time, he always took his tea British-style (steeped in hot water, as opposed to the Indian way, steeped with spices in hot milk) and observed the Queen's teatime in our house for years.

Though my father has to go slowly and tires easily, I am eager for the opportunity to have some form of exercise myself. I do, however, feel mighty self-conscious wearing what, in my Western eyes, are modest-length workout shorts. "I'm not what you think I am!" I want to say to everyone. "I'm a respectful girl. I'm not trampling on your values. Please don't think I am one of those spoiled Americans whose parents didn't raise them right."

This painful self-consciousness does not really exist anywhere in my life anymore except around other Indian people, Indian people who are total strangers. For example, the man who runs the tiny "Indo-Pak Grocery" near my house in the suburbs of Houston—every time I go in, I'm certain that he's judging me for my accent, my mish-mashed Hindi, my Western ways, and my lack of a husband. Of course, he delights over Jill when she goes in on her own to buy things I have taught her to love. She is exactly what she is supposed to be, a lovely, blond, Western woman with a pleasant, respectful demeanor and a taste for spicy food. But I, I am not supposed to ask questions, I am supposed to know how to navigate this place. Sometimes he double-checks and says "Are you sure you want this?" in English, as if it's clear to everyone that I don't know what I'm doing.

The most difficult thing about being an American in India is not simply the shocking, abject poverty all around you, but the attitudes toward that poverty. While it's easy to assume that wealthy Indians find a way to inure themselves to the destitute families who live in the streets below their fancy apartment buildings, and justify their own inaction with "This is the way that it is," so that they do not have to feel pulled to do anything about it, what's surprising is the extent to which the poor themselves have bought into this idea.

For all of the things I love about it, and for all of the bullshit it, like pretty much every religion, has helped justify, perhaps the most frustrating thing for me about Hinduism is the way that is helps maintain a *laissez-faire* attitude toward social justice in India. My father and I discuss this on our walk, the aggravation borne out of attempts to help people who refused help because they felt it was their karmic fate to suffer in this life (and, conversely, that they would be rewarded in future lives for having borne such suffering so well). One of the ways America had changed him, my father muses, was giving him the eyes to see such suffering for what it really is.

"You really see there," he says, as we rounded the perimeter of a playground, "the importance of every human being. Here it's not like that. You take it all for granted."

It's true. You basically have to steel yourself for it just on the walk from my family's building to the car, a mere dozen yards in the dirt. You cannot imagine the shocking disparity in quality of life displayed all around you, bald-faced, monstrous. How do you walk past this every day and live with yourself?

"This is why they never have any change," my father says. "Only very recently have you seen things like charities being started here, people helping the homeless, the sick—and mostly that's brought in by Christians, or by Indians who have lived in the West. Because these people themselves believe it's their duty to endure the sufferings of this life so they will have better karma in the next life."

Papa wears himself out walking, gets lost, and hails a cab to take us back home. "I believe in reincarnation," he tells me, "And I hope that I have lived well enough in this life to earn a good life the next time around. But the way this belief is used to keep people from improving their own lives—it isn't right."

If I were directing this scene, I'd have the screen blur in this moment, zoom in on the somewhat bewildered main character who didn't know that her father believed in reincarnation until he said so. She has made it twenty-three years into her life without bothering to find out what her own father thinks happens after death. Silently, she vows to listen to him more, ask him more questions, pay better attention. This scene is made all the more poignant for audiences when her father later dies.

In Amritsar, my father's hometown in the state of Punjab, we tour the places where he grew up. We're in the cab, and dad is directing the cab-driver with an ease that shocks my mother and me. This is the same man who has gotten us lost on every family vacation in memory? Whose refusal to ask for directions beats all form of male stereotypes and has led to more than one nasty Subhash and Veena fight? I learned how to read a map out of necessity, once I became old enough to sit in the front seat and serve as co-pilot. "Dad, turn here." "Yes, I'm *sure*."

We pull up in front of his old elementary school. I can't place the look on my father's face; I think it is something akin to wonder. He takes me into the courtyard of what's now a very modern-looking campus complete with new basketball courts and volleyball nets.

"I used to study so hard," he tells me. "When we had our exams at the end of the year, I got recognized for being one of the best in the whole school."

"Papa, you were little!" I try to picture my father as a little boy; I am shocked and amazed that I have never done this before.

"Yeah. That was a long time ago."

Eventually, my father's education carried him out of Amritsar—an education made available to him by the imperialist hand which built not only railroad tracks and resentment but also schools, good ones, stretching even to nowhere places like my father's hometown. My father's intelligence and willingness made him well-suited for the disciplined, orderly systems of hard work and advancement which the Indian public schools promised. He wasn't the most imaginative thinker—creative enough to be a good problem solver, certainly—but not wild or fanciful. So I find it surprising that he didn't just settle for the good life, that his ambition and courage pushed him to leave the familiar behind.

He decided to come to America deliberately, even though it was easier then for Indians to gain entry into Britain than the States. When he was my age, in his early twenties, many of his friends were traveling to London for their advanced degrees. Since the British had implemented their system of schooling throughout India, it was easier to match up transcripts and receive credit for classes already taken. American colleges and universities, on the other hand, often made it very difficult for immigrant students to transfer credits. My father ended up spending the first semester of his MBA making up courses he had already taken, and my mother was forced to re-do her Master's degree altogether; her "foreign" M. Ed. was not properly accredited, and therefore unacceptable.

Still, they came to America, and my father never regretted that decision. "In Britain," he told me, "we heard from friends that they weren't treated well there. The British felt so superior and wouldn't give good jobs to Indians. People who should have been doctors became taxi-drivers. I didn't want that kind of life. What would be the point of leaving India in the first place?"

The promise of America was the promise of career for career's sake, the freedom to do what you love, versus India's culture of duty and obligation, doing what you are supposed to do according to your family. Ironically, of course, some of the latter sensibility bled into my own upbringing as first-generation daughter caught between two cultures. But still, we are better at disappointing people in America. In India, as one of my cousins put it, "everybody's running around trying to do things for other people and nobody's happy."

I don't really speak Hindi. It is the only way, and I mean this truly, apart from melodrama it may connote, in which I feel at all like a failure in life. I can understand a great deal of Hindi when spoken to, I know my colors and numbers and animals and foods, but I can only form the most basic sentences of my own in response. The alphabet I recognize, and I can sound out words phonetically but my vocabulary isn't so great and my writing ability is limited to signing my own name.

I can hear my mother: "I know, I know, we screwed up big time!" My one big wish, that they had taught me Hindi when I was a baby. They didn't because they thought it would be best. Raising a child period is uncertain enough, let alone raising one in a completely foreign country. My parents feared that difference would haunt me, that I would be teased, encumbered by an accent. For them, their voices were the main channels through which they encountered resistance, were flagged as "other."

"Can you repeat that?"

"Say, what kinda accent is that?"

"Where on Earth are you from?"

All uttered, of course, by heavily inflected Southern tongues.

The questioning irked my father more than it did my mom. "How long do I have to live here before...?" And so English was my first language. It fact, it was the *only* language they spoke to me, around me, for a long time. By the time I was old enough to wish for bilinguality, to request that my parents start speaking Hindi around the house, they were rusty, throwing in English words where their vocabularies had gone soft. I was in college by the time I figured out that my father was actually *trilingual* (Punjabi), my mother an impressive quad (Punjabi and Urdu). No need to worry about this daughter's assimilation: I'm an all-American, English-only speaker.

I took one semester of Hindi in college, and struggled through the whole thing. Perhaps it was the case of a naturally gifted student bucking up against something, for once, *not* coming naturally. Perhaps I thought, of all things, this should. I've also always been so totally intimidated by other Indian kids, to tell the truth, as if they are part of some club I just don't belong to. They watch Hindi movies, they have spent multiple summers in India, they hang out almost exclusively with other Indians. They knew much more of the language than I did. Me? I took a geeky, dead language (Latin) in high school and have a terrible ear for accents and intricacies. Thank goodness I took that class pass/fail. Needless to say, I did not go back for Hindi 102.

When we started planning our India trip, though, I decided to give Hindi another whirl. I found a set of those ubiquitous Rosetta Stone CD-ROMs on eBay and asked my parents if they would buy them for my birthday, which they of course did. I gave myself a daily schedule and did well with expanding my verbal grasp of Hindi—though I'm still so self-conscious about my terrible accent—and the practice made my three weeks in India a fertile time for my brain to absorb everything I heard. I found myself laughing at jokes, having mostly understood them, and even dreaming in Hindi for weeks after we got back. Dreaming in another language is one of the most sublime things I have ever experienced, as if the gods have favored you: *My child, you are authentic now.*

But it didn't last. My father died, and somehow the desire to work on my Hindi died with him. Losing him only highlighted how much I wish I spoke this language, how inadequate I feel not speaking it, how utterly defeated I am by the whole thing. All of it bundled up too close together. Every six months or so, I reboot those old CDs, still convinced that it's never going to work, wondering if I really want this or if I'm way too accustomed by now to the meaning

I've constructed around it. I'm way past the native-speaker window and ashamed, worried I seem like a fraud, miscast, like a white girl parading around in brown skin.

When I read over my journal from India, I notice the same strange tone—as if I were narrating a BBC documentary instead of writing about my own life. In India, I felt so completely separated from my other life. In India, I did not spend a single moment alone, and I was okay with that; I slept in the same bed as my parents for the first time in many, many years, and it was kind of nice. Everything felt disparate and I didn't know what to do about it. In India, there was nothing to anchor my other life, and nothing to anchor my time in India to my life back home.

My parents echoed this sentiment in a conversation we had in a cab in New Delhi; we were spending our first time alone as a family of three after several days of intense extended-family time, and we were giddy from the freedom, visiting museums, even going to Pizza Hut (someplace we would never go in America) just to eat something that wasn't Indian food. In the restaurant, the most random soundtrack of music on repeat: "Hotel California," "Quit Playing Games With My Heart," "I Just Called To Say 'I Love You,'" & the *Mission Impossible* theme song—Western cultural appropriation in a nutshell.

When my father asked me "What's different?" it was easy to tell him how I and my perspectives had changed. But what I wasn't prepared for was my parents admitting that they didn't feel they fit in India anymore themselves.

"There's a reason we went to America in the first place," my father said. "I'm not sure I would have identified it at the time, but I guess it's because I didn't fit here. Things in America—beliefs, way of life—just made more sense."

"Of course, there are still moments of disconnect," he added—perhaps attributable to the fact that my parents spent their childhoods in such radically different places than where they live now, an experience I'll never be able to relate to.

Here I was always thinking it was *me* who had to straddle the hyphen, me who was busy living in two worlds and not knowing exactly how to do it. Well, at least I was born in America. At least my accent sounds right on one side of the hyphen. Turns out I'm not the only one who doesn't quite fit where I'm supposed to.

Sometimes I miss the sensation of driving through chaos, attempting to follow with my eyes what seemed like indiscernible lanes and crossings. After enough trips out shopping and running errands, I finally understood why Indian addresses include seemingly ridiculous additions like "across the street from ____ bank" or "next to ____ shop." The mailman must need all the help he can get.

India is pure sensory overload, the stretches of possibility baffling: so many humans, so many simultaneous stories, joy, heartache, excrement, beauty. The shanties that are piled impossibly high, laundry strung across lines attached seemingly to nothing, the barefoot little girls who beg at car windows hawking homemade charms to rid your house of the evil eye—*lal mirchi* (red pepper) strung with *nimbu* (lime). I remember wanting to bring them home, wash their dusty feet. Minutes away, posh shopping districts gleam with all the West has to offer: jewelers, Nike, Adidas, KFC. Drive in the right direction and mountains of lush green bloom in the background, accompanied by the sharp smell of the seashore. And beautiful older apartment buildings appear with elaborate art-deco style wrought-iron balconies, pastry shops with pink awnings.

I have always been a people watcher, and India beat airport terminals, gay bars, even Las Vegas for the best people watching. Nowhere else has such an incredible smattering of men and women enacting their various modes of affluence, religion, Westernization, and the corresponding dress. I even managed to spot a woman on the back of a scooter, holding onto the driver, who was most likely her husband, dressed in both a sari and a baseball cap: not my grandmother's India.

Still, there are some things that remain the same. Nothing's more "old school" than shopping with capable women, watching them inspect seams, examine goods, haggle for a fair price, flirt and argue with salesmen. I think of my Varsha Bhabi, the queen of efficient competency, whose smile still radiates the same unique beauty I have seen in her wedding pictures. I find myself clucking my tongue along with her and my mother, *"Nehi, nehi"* dismissing inferior saris with the wave of a hand. There are all kinds of cultural markers and indicators strung together—one way to say "thank you" to a Muslim, another to a Hindu. India is an old, old place, no one is particularly in a hurry, everything is negotiable, and everyone is a storyteller.

My father took care of business as if he knew. While in India, my parents made countless gifts of things: jewelry, money, saris. They even signed over the lease of a flat they had held all those years, in which they let my father's sister live for free. She had had a hard go of things—was married to an abusive husband and struggled to provide for her two boys after divorcing him. My father wanted her to own something of her own, to say that the place where she lived belonged to her.

We spent part of an afternoon at the district court, a sprawling building set seemingly in the middle of nowhere, painted a bright turquoise. People piled up, waiting—all of India assembled, as if at a train station. My mother and I telling stories in a corner while we waited for the molasses systems of justice to do their thing.

Here is where I'd like my little film to end: in a building I could not locate on a map, on a day when I had no obligations or appointments of my own, standing someplace I'll never be again, catching my father's eye from where he stood at the top of the stairs, handsome with his beard and his grin, feet in leather *chappals*, hairy legs peeking out from his shorts, very much alive and walking toward me.

4

Sonata

I.

For months, the movie screen of my mind featured the same scene—my father's face against a white hospital sheet—over and over and over again. Skin turns sallow and loses elasticity remarkably fast. Either a body is living or it is not.

II.

My father was a hairy man, one of those hairy men. I think women who don't mind hairy men had hairy men for dads. My dad's back was pretty smooth, which helped, but his arms and legs were curly and crowded with hair. Each day he was in the hospital, I would put lotion on for him. First because he asked, then because I would suggest, finally because it was a continuation, a habit, an enactment of the belief that it mattered whether or not his skin was dry. His hair would become tangled and twisted as I tried to rub the lotion in, until I smoothed it in one direction with the inside of my palm, the way a vacuum cleaner shades carpet into even rows.

Tending to one's parent is tricky. I remember when I stopped sleeping in the same bed as my mother—it wasn't what we did every night, but maybe once a week or so. As I got older, less frequently. Once I started sleeping in beds with other people, I couldn't sleep next to my mother anymore. The lines felt too blurry. I didn't say this to her. I told her I felt like I had "grown out of it." She had a hard time with that.

Someday, I will know what it feels like to delight completely in my grown child. I saw pride in my father's face, even in that oddest of times. "I'll need you to pay the bills online." Far from the days of macaroni necklaces and tempera-paint handprints, I was proving my salt.

III.

It happened on a regular Saturday. Someone's Sabbath, someone's tailgate, someone's first piano recital or first sushi or first time to watch *On the Waterfront*. My father's first and only death.

We had arranged for Saturday to be visitation day, something to placate everyone calling our house, calling my cell phone, "How is Subhash?" Our doctor had told us the Wednesday before that we didn't have much time. On Friday, my day alone with him, I told him, "If you could just make it until Saturday, okay Papa? That's when everyone's coming to see you. After that, you just do what you need to do." I was past the point of caring whether he could hear me or not.

I told the doctor, "We want to place a DNR," just like I learned to do from the movies and from television shows. I even got the empathy and a silent nod that I hoped meant, "You're doing the right thing." One part surprised me, though. There was no paperwork to sign. All I had to do was say *don't bring my father back to life* and they changed his wristband to a different color: orange, meaning no heroic measures.

IV.

Varsha somehow got away from her fancy New York law firm job to fly home for twenty-four hours. She is like my little sister; our families have known each other since before we were born. I remember her walking out into the lobby from the ICU and wiping her eyes with the sleeve of her blue Carolina Tarheels sweatshirt. There is so much of Varsha in my memory, the little fountain ponytail she used to sport on the top of her head as a toddler, her childhood and preteen obsession with miniature perfume bottles, the ups and downs of her relationship with the long-distance and long-term boyfriend she will soon marry. But those tears, they caught me off guard. As if they proved what was happening, that someone, my father, was about to die for real.

Varsha was promptly given a yellow legal pad and placed in charge of listing the visitors who showed up for the rest of the day, so that my mother and I might thank them later. One of death's many, slightly perverse rituals: lots and lots of thank-you notes.

"But how can I write down their names if I don't *know* their names?" Varsha protested with a half-sheepish, half-pleading face. It's true, none of us kids do. That's one of the hallmarks of our extended Indian immigrant community structure—everyone is "Uncle" or "Aunty," even people you have known your whole life—leaving you clueless as to their actual first or last names. These titles are lovely and familiar, but not very helpful on a sign-in sheet. So whenever brown people appeared from the third-floor elevators, we figured they belonged to us, and Varsha would ask them to please sign in. By the end of the day, the top sheet of the legal pad was full. Word travels quickly, and even people who had pinched my cheeks the last time they saw me were showing up.

While my mother sat, balled up tight, at my father's side, I stayed in the waiting room, trying to hide, reading fluffy magazines with my friend Kristen. She sat next to me and held my Starbucks cup every time I got up to hug someone, or let them hug me. As the hours passed, Kristen became my homing device, her body soft and round next to mine, the smell of her wet hair familiar. Even her nickname for me, "Nini," began to sound like a wise and profound benediction. I could not bear the look she was giving me, the awfulness of the situation mirrored in her eyes, so I read aloud an article about a woman who was addicted to calling psychic hotlines, in the way that as victims we will inversely seek to comfort those who are there to comfort us, distract them, reassure them that we are alright. This woman in the article had written a book, *Psychic Junkie*, and its title made Kristen laugh like I knew it would, her unbelievably loud laugh startling the room, a belly laugh she inherited from her father.

A couple whom I knew by face but not by name approached. Kristen elbowed me subtly, and I got up. The woman reminded me a little bit of my mom, the way she looks in old pictures with long hair, light skin, and almond eyes. Her husband was wearing a denim shirt which pulled at his broad shoulders. His head was perfectly round and covered with thinning salt-and-pepper hair. Both of their faces betrayed the shock of having just seen my father, who just a few weeks before had shown no traces of illness. I braced myself for another exchange with well-meaning but frustrating people, the good girl in me ready to smile and cut them some slack, the angry woman in me tired of hugs, of useless comfort, of having to swallow platitudes. The usual blur of words occurred: "Oh, sweetheart… so sad…how are you?…take care of your mother," etc. They asked questions about what the doctors were saying, as if I had the energy to go over details, and suggested various avenues of investigation, as if they were going to find the magic solution that dozens of experts had missed. Before my face could betray my frustration, I issued the standard "Thank you for coming," in a tone like the lights coming on in a bar at 2 a.m. Then the man looked at me gravely, nodding his head for emphasis and said, "We believe that miracles happen everyday. We pray for that."

V.

FOR THE RECORD: The only good things to say to someone experiencing a terrible loss are "I love you" and "I'm sorry." Please do not tell them that things happen for a reason, that their loved one will now be an angel in heaven looking over them, that this experience will make them stronger, or that you understand how they feel. You don't.

VI.

My mother and I fought. Of course we did. That is the thing no one ever seems to mention; she yelled and I pushed. Apparently it happens all the time. That part I hope my father couldn't hear.

Around five o'clock on visiting day, after the crowds had come and gone, Gloria, my father's day nurse came to me and said "His blood pressure has been falling steadily all day. I don't think he's going to make it through the night." I told Kristen, who left me reluctantly, with a big squeeze and a solemn face. My mother drove home and brought back her Sanskrit prayer books, my English copy of the *Bhagavad Gita*, and *Charlotte's Web*. We sat on either side of the bed and I held my father's hand while Mom read her prayers aloud. It occurred to me then that there was a part of my father I would never know, since I had not learned to speak to him in his first language. I sang along with my mother in the places I knew by heart.

First, we asked the nurses to stop increasing his Levophed, which regulated his blood pressure: too much of the medicine and his kidneys would fail. We asked them to stop pricking his finger every hour to check his blood sugar. At our request, they took the pressure stockings off of his legs, and I could see how swollen his feet were. Finally, we asked Katie, who had the night shift, to stop giving him Levophed altogether. His blood pressure fell, but then leveled again. He had two weeks' worth of heavy meds in his body.

Hours passed and the room grew dark. Charlotte had saved Wilbur, and then died. I decided that when I die, I want someone to say about me what is said of Charlotte at the very end: "It is not often that someone comes along who is a true friend and a good writer. Charlotte was both." The respirator kept regular time, its electric blue tubing shaking slightly with each forced breath. My father had been attached to the thing, officially considered a heroic measure, for a week and three days. His doctor had told me, frankly, that there was no way he would last on his own without it. "A few minutes, maybe."

My mother wasn't prepared, that goes without saying. Because how do you really prepare for something like this? But we had discussed things, we had agreed that my father would want a dignified death. Not the drama of cardiac arrest, or the tragedy of kidney failure. This was our plan: failing all else, we would take my father off the respirator on Tuesday, an auspicious day for my family. Most Hindu families observe a holy day that corresponds with the god that the household primarily worships. My father, a man who so loved his food, even gave up meat once a week, every week, on that day. My mother and I felt that Tuesday would only be fitting. But that was in theory, on paper, and not in practice. So when it became clear that we did not have until Tuesday, my mother, who likes her plans, her color-coded files, her control, who passed on to me her habit of subdividing her grocery lists to match the layout of the store's aisles, balled up again, tight and unwilling to budge. And so, I pushed.

I pushed because I was exhausted, waiting for my father to die. I pushed because I could not stand to watch him a minute longer, full of tubes and wires with his goddamn blood pressure alarm beeping every fifteen minutes. I pushed because I knew what he would want, and I wanted to give him that: if nothing else, a peaceful passing. I pushed because I was not about to leave that room, was not about to go home and wait for a phone call, could not bear the thought of my father dying alone like Charlotte. I pushed because I knew my father was going to die, but you can't start grieving for it until it happens. I pushed. I don't regret it.

My mother said harsh things, things I wish I did not remember.

"Why are you being so impatient?"

"You just want to do what's easier for you."

"This is how you have always been—completely selfish."

"So, what, you *want* him to die?"

I don't think she has any memory of being this way, nor did her words wound me, her desperation was so clear. I held the party line as quietly as I could. It didn't take long for her anger to push in and through and out the other side of her fear. "I can't do it," she wailed. "I know I should but I can't."

"It's okay, Momma. You don't have to." I stepped out into the hall, where the nurse supervisor promised me again that morphine would ensure that my father felt no pain when his life left his body. How can anyone make a promise like that? Of course, it was the one I wanted. "Please," I said to her. "Now."

VII.

CONFESSION: My brain did not stop running, even when my father was dying. The one time you would think I wouldn't have to scream to myself "Pay attention!" but there it all was, bad commercial jingles and song lyrics and even the question, "When is this going to end?" I felt the strangeness of time, and tried to will my father out of being.

VIII.

The respiratory technician was a tall, thin man with lovely dark skin, much darker than mine, like a coffee bean. His fingers were long, I remember that. I watched him unhook the respirator tube and attach another, connected to an oxygen tank. I think it took about two minutes for my father to die, with me sitting on my mother's lap, my face buried in my father's side. "Let go, Papa, let go."

Katie, our tiny nurse, had curly hair and a wedding ring. Her diamond surprised me, I guess because she looked like a sixteen-year-old. She turned off the alarms on the screen which monitored my father's heartbeat, oxygen level, and blood pressure, and stood at the back of the room and cried while my father died. I loved her for crying. Her eyes were so red when I said goodbye to her. I don't remember looking in the mirror at myself that night when I got home, but I imagine her face when I think about how I felt. Quiet and empty.

At the end, you do have to sign paperwork, a release form. I must say, I did it beautifully, no tears on the clipboard, no melodrama. The inside of my chest burned as if it had been scraped hollow with a soup spoon, like a pumpkin at Halloween. I went back to pick up my purse and kissed his forehead which was already so foreign and so cold. "My father is a body now," I thought, and walked away.

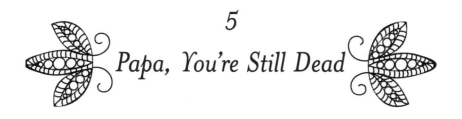

5
Papa, You're Still Dead

Be strong, They say. Be brave. Be a rock. Don't cry. Cry if you need to. Everything's going to be fine. Don't worry. These things make you stronger. It's better this way. He's in a better place now. I'm sorry, but everything happens for a reason. We're praying for him. He'll be fine, They say. Now you have an angel looking down on you from heaven. At least he lived a good life. At least he didn't suffer. He knew how much you loved him. He'll always be with you. You didn't really lose him, They say. He lives *in* you. Don't cry. It will be okay. Time heals all things, They say. Just give it time.

The night my father died, I crawled into the four-poster, canopy bed that had been the pride of my childhood and which remained, until very recently, in my childhood home. Lying there, looking up at the glow-in-the-dark plastic stars I had long-ago affixed to the metal "ribs" that hold up the canopy fabric, I dialed the dozen numbers attached to my partner Jill's international cell phone. She had left the country on a business trip two weeks prior with my blessing, back when my father was still with us, still with it. Though he had been in the hospital at the time, there was absolutely no indication that his condition was even close to terminal, so she went. By the time everything changed, the only flight Air France had to offer would have returned her to the States just a few hours sooner than she was already scheduled to arrive, and would have cost $1700.

So the night—or rather, the very early morning—after I watched my father die, I called across the planet ten thousand miles away to share the news out loud, the first of many times that I would say, "My father is dead." I did not cry on the phone; my head felt dark and fuzzy and out of tears. My room seemed to be floating somewhere encapsulated, like the dreams I had as a child where my wondrous bed turned into a magical raft and transported me to fabulous places. This time, the fabulous place was Istanbul, from whence Jill's voice poured in with sunlight, a market bazaar and heady spices sifting out through the end of the phone. Blue Mosque, Turkish sky, half Europe and half Asia, all sunglasses and cotton, light against hot skin. In my imagining, the film of my life opened up into a split screen with me, blanket, and covers on one side and she, sunglasses, and worry on the other.

"There's a pigeon," she told me. "A fat one. He's sitting on top of this fountain next to the mosque—there's some kind of iron curlicue flourish and he's barely balancing his weight on top of it. His fat is bulging out on the sides. He says the Ottomans put this fountain here just for him to sit on top of and be beautiful."

Somehow this was the most comforting thing she could have possibly said.

"Of course they did," I replied.

"Just think about him, sweetheart," she said. "And try to get some sleep."

And then the movie screen joined up again, scrolling to one side, with the light disappearing, leaving behind my dark childhood bedroom and the phantom beeping of hospital machines that would sound in my head for weeks to come.

As with other life-altering experiences (one thinks of becoming a parent or falling in love), words often fail when attempting to describe or categorize grief. The classical Greeks, for example, seem not to have had a word for grief other than the word they used for pain. In the modern world, philosophers and behaviorists have attempted to prove by logic what most of us know by instinct: that grief is an emotional experience unto itself. There is nothing like it. And while it may seem pointless to attempt to quantify something we all agree is impossible to describe, the way that scientists think about grief may actually prove useful to those of us experiencing it. To dissect and examine that which plagues us can bring understanding, if not quite relief. Better the devil that you know, and so forth.

Grief is, no doubt, an emotional experience. In fact, it is almost its own emotional category, since grief encompasses so many other emotions within itself: sadness, anger, fear, confusion, etc. There are two major categories of emotions, according to the people who decide these things: cognitive and conative. Conative feelings are those that arise from instinct. A pleasurable physical sensation or a rush of sudden fear both bypass our cognitive mechanisms: we don't need to think in order to experience them. Cognitive emotions, then, are the ones *dependent* upon our capacity to think. Jealousy can only arise if we first identify that someone else has something we want; as quickly as it may occur, this is still cognition.

Grief is an odd duck because it is both cognitive and conative. That old maxim, "Grief is not rational," is a rather pithy summary of the conative aspects of grief. While cognitive emotions are subject to rationality, conative emotions are unmoved by human attempts to rationalize. For example, when I realize that being angry with my boss (a cognitive emotion) is making me dread going to work every day and hurting *me* more than my boss, my anger may lessen. But no amount of physical evidence or rational assertions will keep me from feeling terror (conative) when I wake up in the middle of the night to a loud THUMP! I have no cognitive access to that terror; it comes up whether it is warranted or not. To be fair, cognitive emotions are also sometimes subject to irrationality, simply because we are human and often mistaken in our thinking. A young woman may be filled with joy because she just *knows* that her lottery ticket will be the lucky one. Is her joy irrational? Most of us would say so.

But joy as an emotion is still cognitive, because it is dependent upon a belief, however misguided that belief might be.

Though conative emotions could be labeled "irrational," I think it's more accurate to say that they fall outside of the realms of rationality or irrationality. I know that my father is dead and will always be dead, but that doesn't stop me from wishing it weren't so. Grief is in fact constituted by irrational desire, the desire that what one knows or believes to be true (i.e. that a certain individual has died) should not be. So as long as I wish that my father were still alive, I am grieving. And under that definition, I believe it is fair to assert that I will grieve forever.

Two days after my father's funeral, Jill was back in the States and in my parents' house. I was, as it turned out, tremendously glad she had not been present for the death and dying business; it was a comfort to be with someone who had come, seemingly, from another world.

I told her the stories of the days that had passed, recounting the events in order to make them more real for myself. I pulled her into the guest bedroom to make love, desperate to feel something, anything else. I used her face as a mirror to see how she would find me changed. I wept, sobbing into her shoulder, many times.

I suggested an outing to see an Annie Leibovitz exhibit at the local art museum. The collection featured portrait photographs of famous musicians, everyone from Iggy Pop to Eminem, and I had been meaning to see it all summer. We drove and parked and bought tickets, as if she were in town for a tourist's weekend, instead of being there to witness my grief and shelter me from it; neither of us knew how things worked now, if we should be acting differently.

The photographs we had come to see hung against carpet-covered walls on the first floor, underground. The space was cold and quiet, save for a video documentary that ran continuously behind a half-wall in the back room. As we walked, Jill and I fell into our own individual paces, drawn to different portraits, occasionally beckoning the other to point out a detail, or answer a question. I have always been a Springsteen fan; she has been in love with Dolly Parton since she was a little girl.

This is what I have always enjoyed about being in an art gallery: the private experience, the stillness and silence. Guided tours do not appeal to me, even the recorded kind. Talkative, hand-holding couples drive me nuts. At least, that is how I was, before. But that day, something new happened. We were halfway through a fascinating exhibit in the cool, dim basement of the Brooks Museum of Art and my heart was racing. My brain, too. Jill and I stood side-by-side in front of Lucinda Williams, who was in jeans and cowboy boots on a dirt road. As Jill turned to move onto the next photograph, I felt a panic in my stomach. A plaintive, pathetic *Don't leave!* formed in my throat. Jill was standing just a half-a-dozen feet away, but I was so anxious not to be alone, even there, even on a patch of carpet in a room full of other people. I felt like I was on an island with no one to hang onto, alone with my brain and its obsessive echolalia: "Your father is dead, your father is dead, your father is dead." I *wanted* talk, I wanted chatter. I wanted Jill to hold my hand, walk me through the gallery, and not let go.

In the weeks following my father's death, I was only partially in reality about what had happened. True, I had been in the room when he took his last breath; I saw his body at the funeral home when the casket was opened for the Hindu priest to perform last rites; I even pushed the button in the crematorium that sent his body, dressed in silk *kurta* pajamas with a silver envelope addressed to "Papa" in his hands, to be burned to ash in accordance with Indian tradition.

Still, it didn't seem real. This is common among mourners, a sense of shock, of disbelief. A kind of cinematic unreality takes over, makes it difficult to process input or generate output. "Should

I get out of bed?" becomes a monumental decision. Distinguishing between what's important and what isn't is no longer possible because nothing seems as important as the fact that someone is dead.

The real trouble with grief as a category of emotion is this: there isn't anything to do. Normally, emotions, whether cognitive or conative, serve as motivators for human behavior. They generate goals and intentions. They give us something to do in response. In the case of grief, however, there are no appropriate actions, nothing that can bring about what the grieving wish for. The desire that one might go back in time that the course of events might be reversed, that a father should come back from the dead—are impossible ones. The normal functions of the emotion-desire-motive matrix are blocked. You can't play your usual tricks with grief. Grief requires an entirely different game plan.

"*I Wasn't Ready To Say Goodbye*; *Letting Go With Love*; *Rainbows and Rain*; *When You Lose Someone You Love*? Um, I don't think so." Following our museum visit, Jill had insisted on a trip to a big-box bookstore so that I could buy a grief book. I was utterly, doggedly resistant to the idea; *those* kind of books weren't for me. I had never purchased a self-help book in my life, and I did not intend to start now. And my resistance was only confirmed and compounded as I reluctantly and half-heartedly browsed through the shelves.

Every book in the "bereavement" section had a generically cheesy picture of a lake or a sunset on the cover. What were these people thinking? My dad might have died, but I hadn't lost my sense of aesthetics. Plus, I was looking for more than thin platitudes or pop psychology, neither of which were going to comfort or empower me. I'll admit that the idea of a book—a field guide, a map—*did* sound kind of good to me. I'm a book person, a writer, someone who believes in research and study, which is of course why the very wise Jill had insisted on my getting a book in the first place. But rigid, clinical outlines of the stages of grief weren't going to work and neither was the bad theology of "trust in God's plan." Where was the grief book for people who didn't like self-help books or go to church? Everybody's father dies, has been dying, has always died, since the beginning of time, so how could it be that we still hadn't figure out what to say about it?

Here are some things those sweet little books don't tell you:

1. Grief is a fickle, quicksilver mistress—wrapped up close to you one minute, gone the next. She might return in a short moment, or she may stay away for days. But she has never truly left for good. She will *always* come back.
2. Grief is completely unpredictable and inconsistent. What triggered it one day will not bother you in the slightest the next. What soothed and brought you comfort last night will offer no help the following morning.
3. Your friends will want to help, but they will have no idea what to do for you. And you won't really be able to tell them.
4. Ninety-nine percent of the people who say "I understand" or "I know how you feel" don't. The ones who do understand know better than to say things like that.
5. Grief brings gifts. You'd never want to say it like that, because it sounds perverse, and there is no good math for equations that involve death, but it's true. Sharp doses of clarity, incredibly intense flashes of gratitude and perspective, a cleansing kind of anger, even ease. Death of a loved one makes everything both more complicated and less complicated, all at once.
6. Time doesn't actually make it better. Time just makes it different.

Grief's effects are not just limited to the mind and the heart. The body also does its level best to mark the drama of the occasion. For many mourners whose minds are shrouded with shock, the physiological effects of bereavement are almost like bruises, marking what has passed. Such indicators further demonstrate grief's conative properties by showing how we are unable to control the physical effects of our emotional experiences; even on a day when we "feel fine," our bodies indicate otherwise.

When you grieve, your brain interprets the loss as a stressor. In a series of seamless reactions, like a chain of dominos, your body activates the endocrine system, which you may remember from high school biology. Should you need a refresher, the endocrine system is essentially your body's regulatory mechanism and oversight committee, those guys sitting in mission control making sure that "All systems are go." And when there is a hitch in the mission, your endocrine system kicks in for damage control, sending hormones where they're needed most. In the case of extreme stress, the hypothalamus sends a messenger hormone to the pituitary gland, which, in turn, produces a second hormone that travels through the bloodstream to the adrenal glands, which sit on top of the kidneys like elf hats. At last, your properly-stimulated adrenal glands give up the goods: cortisol. Ahhhh, that's better.

A quick burst of cortisol feels like a sugar rush, because that's essentially what it is. Glucose gives you energy, heightens your memory functions, lowers your sensitivity to pain, and increases your appetite: all things that prove quite helpful when encountering a stress event like death. The only problem is that, in larger amounts, the short-term benefits of cortisol fail to outweigh the long-term damage it can cause. In order to rev you up, your body has to increase your blood pressure and heart rate, which can wear heavily on cardiovascular health after a while. Cortisol also breaks down bone mass and muscle tissue while scavenging for resources in the body. Worst of all, it suppresses your immune system, in order to save calories. There you are, already under stress, now extra-susceptible to getting sick. Sounds like a design flaw, right? Well, it is an unfortunate give-and-take, but not an entirely unreasonable choice for your body to make. After all, to suppress any other system—your vascular system, or nervous system, for instance—would certainly have an instant, disastrous effect. By temporarily suppressing its immune system, your body is hedging its bet against the chance that you might get sick. Stress is a demand, and it takes its toll.

I can recognize both the short-term and long-term effects of grief from my own experience. One line from a journal entry that summer betrays what must have been the effects of my cortisol high: "When did I turn into a machine with no feelings?" I remember being astounded by my seeming ability to push forward, through hospital business, family business, and funeral business without feeling exhausted or really, feeling anything at all. For about a month I was superwoman, "the rock." Everyone was amazed, and I was grateful that I was able to take care of things when my mother was not able; as someone who carries stress more heavily and consistently than I do, I think she hit her breaking point about two weeks before I did.

But eventually, my body caught up to the state of things and started to act funny: insomnia and hair loss, two things I'd never experienced before in my life, were the big ones. Dryness of the hair, skin, and vaginal area are also common among females under intense stress: so are depression, fatigue, and fluctuation of weight. When it all started happening to me, I felt a little bit like I imagine menopausal women do, watching your body alter outside of your control. Try as I might, my will had no effect over my grief. If my hair was going to fall out, it was going to fall out. All I could do was wait for it to stop.

A feeling is said to be hypercognized when there are many different cross-cultural structures for responding to it, interpreting it, and expressing it. Unlike, for instance, pain or fear, an emotional experience like grief is manifested in different ways across the world.

This suggests that our methods of grieving are taught and learned; perhaps we even teach the very feelings associated with grief. If emotions have adaptive functions, then grief itself developed because it brought a certain value to the group, specifically groups of primates from which human beings evolved. Commemorating a death and participating in the act of grieving have been shown to create bonding between individuals—think of the resurgence of American patriotism in the face of 9/11 or the way that a natural disaster can bring out the best in a small-town community. In fact, no positive reaction or incentive has been shown to promote social cohesiveness the way a powerful bereavement response can.

Unfortunately, what I see in modern-day America is a very schizophrenic culture surrounding death. In the "old school" cultures of the South or within immigrant/minority communities, there is a clear prescription for what to do when someone dies: you make a casserole, you take it over to the house, you sit with the bereaved, you answer the phone and do the things they aren't up to doing yet. You leave some sleeping pills in the medicine cabinet, just in case. You tell stories about the one who was lost.

Yet if we turn to pop culture for cues, we learn instead that we should do everything we can to push *against* death. Shelter children from the sick and the aged, buy disembodied grocery-store meat and grow squeamish at the mention that it once belonged to a living creature, embalm the dead in order to create a "life-like" appearance—the perversity is overwhelming. Death is fundamental to our very nature; it is a constant, a universal, it is the thing that makes life precious. But we are mindful of it in all the wrong ways.

I think of the cultural traditions of India, my homeland. There, as prescribed by religion but also by the social matrix, rituals mark every step of a family's journey in grief. Loud, unbridled emotional responses are expected. Communities immediately mobilize to bring food, keep vigil over the body, consult the priest, pay the necessary costs. Yearly anniversaries of the death event are also marked by rituals. Time limits are not placed on the mourning period for spouses, children, or parents. Life is interrupted, and that interruption is acknowledged instead of suppressed.

Here, the business of death has become precisely that, a business. And it isn't a cheap one, either. We made the arrangements for my father's funeral and subsequent cremation at a family-owned funeral home in Memphis. On Sunday, less than twenty-four hours after my father had died, I sat in a room with my mother, her brother, and two of our family friends, discussing—no, bargaining—over the cost of my father's death. It was the most disgusting display of commerce I have ever witnessed.

Luckily for my mother and me, we were accompanied by two tough, level-headed friends who had been through the funeral racket before. They managed to plod through every last detail, arguing for the things they knew we wanted and driving down the cost wherever possible. Along with the rest of our core community of Indian immigrants, they brought traditions and attitudes that were more welcome than ever in the weeks following my father's death. Mom and I were cared for and supported by a whole crew of people who loved us, and my father. Without asking, they kept our refrigerator stocked with food, paid for my father's funeral expenses, picked up my best friend from the airport, and wrote a very large check as a loan to my mother who was waiting for the paperwork to come through on my father's life insurance. I will never forget, the morning after my father died, waking up in my parents' house to the sound of quiet voices downstairs. Something about the house not being empty, about the witnessing which was being provided, took the edge off of my shock and exhaustion.

But right there along with the incredible gestures of thoughtfulness and generosity came the terribly misguided ones. Hearing that my father is now an angel looking down on me from heaven is about the farthest thing from comforting that I can imagine hearing. "You need to be strong," I was told at least a dozen times. Others were so visibly uncomfortable in the presence of my grief that they would inanely repeat "It's going to be okay," when it clearly was not. I realize that comforting the bereaved is a no-win situation; you want so desperately to ease their suffering, but there is no way to do so. There is, in short, really nothing good to say except "I love you" and "I'm sorry." But would it be so hard to acknowledge that? Would it be so difficult to acknowledge another person's suffering instead of trying to smooth it away? What concerns me about my experiences as a griever is how difficult it is for us in this culture to be with someone's pain. We tell our children, "Don't cry," even though sometimes that is precisely what they need to do. Hurt must be expressed, or it only increases.

I've never felt anything like this in my entire life; nothing close. Songs and movies and television shows prepared me (even if with a somewhat skewed perspective) for what it would feel like to fall in love, to feel sexual desire, to be annoyed with my parents, to live the college life, to have my heart broken. But nowhere did anyone ever tell me that losing a parent would be the most devastating, earth-shattering, life-altering thing that would happen to me.

Three months after my father died, I volunteered to participate in a study, the aim of which was to catalogue the coping mechanisms employed by individuals experiencing severe distress. After an initial meeting with Ben, the psychology graduate student running the study, I was given a series of computerized surveys designed to measure my current level of distress and determine which, if any, coping mechanisms I had used up to that point. Then, for twenty-one days following, I took an online survey each night, answering thirty-five questions before I went to bed. Clicking on the appropriate bubble, I first told the computer the degree to which I had felt certain emotions that day, including "proud," "excited," "worthless," and "sad." Then, I responded to the last fifteen questions, indicating what I had done in response to any negative feelings I had experienced that day. Among those choices were "distracted myself from negative feelings," "asked people in my life for assurance that I am worthwhile," "tried to push negative feelings away."

Always a fan of research and hard-working graduate students, I diligently completed my survey each night. Following a two-day break, I took a short series of exit surveys and then met with Ben the next day to collect my nominal participation fee and learn more about the study. With dark, thinning hair and a small silver earring, Ben was probably in his late twenties or early thirties. He spoke English with a continental accent (his birth country is Turkey) and his handsomeness made me a bit self-conscious, as did the knowledge that he had access to data concerning my emotional state for the previous three weeks. Soon, however, I found myself on common ground with him, eager to hear about the impetus behind his research.

"The hypothesis we're operating on is basically this: individuals who attempt to distract themselves from or avoid the negative emotions in their life will ultimately experience a rebound effect. That is, those negative feelings will get worse if pushed away. What we're looking for is a spike in the data, about a day or two after an individual has reported behavior like ignoring negative thoughts or trying to think about something else. If our hypothesis is correct, a spike will show up in the self-reported emotions data, in the feelings like worthlessness and sorrow." He spoke with his hands, gesturing as if drawing graphs in the air.

"And has that been what you've found so far? Are you allowed to tell me that?"

He smiled. "Sure. I mean, yes. We—I—have a lot of data to plot, but so far it's confirming what we hoped."

"Congratulations," I said.

"Thank you. And thank you for remembering to do your survey every night. Here we go." He handed me twenty-five dollars in cash. I grabbed my bag and made my way towards the door.

"Ben, what made you choose this topic in the first place?"

"Well, I guess I hope that the conclusions we'll reach here will help care-providers realize that it's better for their patients and clients to fully express their emotions, even the negative ones."

"I think that is so important—I just feel really strongly about it since my dad died—people keep offering me medication, trying to distract me, but…I feel like I should feel it. I mean, my dad died. It should be difficult, right?"

"You are brave," he said. "It is a good thing."

"Thank you," I said, blushing. I halfway wanted to kiss him, but we were standing in the middle of a busy university hallway. Instead, he shook my hand, and I left.

Eventually, I did come across I grief book I found palatable. *Healing Your Grieving Heart: 100 Practical Ideas* bears a less than stellar title, but a very simple, unoffensive line drawing of an oak tree on the cover. What drew me to it and kept me engaged in it were the simple suggestions and affirmations on every page. Number 13: Cry, Number 52: Take a Risk, Number 81: Schedule Something That Gives You Pleasure Each Day. When your brain feels like that of an early Alzheimer's patient, easily confused and overwhelmed, simple directions and dictations are a blessing. I felt like I was like the extreme sports version of what the Buddhists call "monkey mind"— because instead of a monkey, swinging from thought to thought, I had a black hole in my brain. Construction of a decision, a sentence, a rational thought, were all doomed from the start. "Should I make a cup of tea?" felt like a life-altering question to be asking, and one I found difficult to answer, despite being aware of how ridiculous the whole situation was. Luckily, when I wasn't feeling completely humiliated by my lack of ability to function in the world, I found it all pretty hilarious.

For example: I bought a shower curtain. Following the suggestion of Number 43: Go Shopping, I decided that I would go on a little spree to liven up my living space. My operating principle: buy whatever within my budget would make me happy, no matter how temporary the happiness or how frivolous the purchase. Hence, the shower curtain, discovered on clearance, in bright pink canvas, complete with two ridiculous pockets. Pleased as punch, I spent twelve whole dollars on the thing before tromping back to my car, where I promptly realized that the shower in my apartment, where I had lived for over six months, had doors. Sliding, glass doors.

Another distinct memory: the first day of classes, my second year of graduate school, almost exactly a month after my father's death. I was taking a poetry craft seminar, and at that first meeting we were all asked to go around the table and state our name, concentration, and something that interested us as writers. I was the last one to share.

In the fifteen or so minutes it took to make these introductions, I felt myself grow incredibly, unpredictably, and uncharacteristically pissed off. It was all I could do not to leap across the table and strangle some of the most pretentious students as they spoke. "Well, I'm occupied with deconstructing the ontological premises of life and getting down beneath that to what's real. My work is informed primarily by Foucault and obscure Polynesian tribal myth."

I'm the first one to admit, had it been any other day, any other time, I would have probably tried just as hard to impress everybody as they did. But within the razor-edge context of grief, all I could think was, *You poor, sad, ridiculous people.* When I wasn't hating them all, I felt sorry for them, not even superior, just numb and tired. *All of this matters not, you fools, and you have absolutely no idea.* The whole thing was laughable.

When my turn came around, I said the most honest and nonjudgmental thing I could muster: "My name is Nishta, I write non-fiction, and my father just died. I really have no idea what I'm interested in, I'm just proud of myself for taking a shower today."

In the months that followed, I managed to get things a little bit more together. I made my way to the Student Health Center and found myself a grief counselor who listened to me once a week with patient detachment and told me that everything I was experiencing was completely normal. (When you feel like you may be losing your mind, "normal" becomes the most comforting word imaginable.) I filled my tiny graduate school apartment with pictures of my father, collaged in the days after he had died. Every few weeks, I sat down to write him a letter on special stationary. I created my own rituals, enlisting the support and participation of my friends. For Diwali, the Hindu New Year, I spent hours making all of my Dad's favorite Indian foods (with plenty of consultation calls to my mother) and then invited hungry graduate students over to celebrate with me. That Thanksgiving, a table full of people who, Jill being the exception, had never met my father, toasted to his memory. My hair stopped falling out in clumps. I got my libido back. I no longer needed "Organic Nighty Night" tea to help me get to sleep. My daily life no longer revolved around grieving, although grief was certainly present. Then and now, over five years later, grief still shows up and brings me to my knees. And there still isn't anything I can do about it.

"You just find a place to put it," was the most helpful thing anyone ever said to me about grief. "It doesn't go away, you don't wake up one day, finished with your grieving. You just make a space for it, and the fit becomes less and less uncomfortable." How I wish that were the message being sold in bookstores, instead of soaring eagles and sunsets.

My entire life has been thrown into sharp relief since my father's death. I think of *The Iliad*, of Achilles' rage over the death of his beloved Patroclus, dragging the body of poor Hector in circles for days, though he knows it will never bring his cousin back. And of Priam, an old man who sets aside his pride and fear to sneak across enemy lines and beg for the body of his son. Their motivator is a grief which I now understand.

Earlier today, at an airport terminal, I heard a young woman say "Daddy!" into her phone, and in my brain I heard a sound like an angry game show buzzer, those little red Xs that flash across the screen whenever a contestant answers incorrectly. *Oh Papa*, I thought, *I'm on a plane to Houston and you're still dead.*

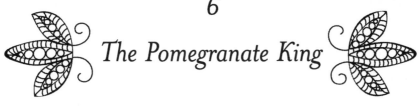

6

The Pomegranate King

Pomegranates are indigenous to the middle world, that strait of land we now call Iran, which reaches its shoulder up into the Mediterranean and bumping its back side into Pakistan. From this Fertile Crescent the fruit traveled, through accidental and purposeful means of cultivation, both east and west, dropping its fine seed into the dry, deep soil of Turkey, Afghanistan, and India. One thinks of camels, brightly colored silks, young slaves, and bundles of curled cinnamon.

It is not difficult to understand why some ancient soul would dare to smash and chance the first pomegranate. Unlike, say, the artichoke or the durian, the pomegranate advertises itself well in its natural state. Green, waxy leaves about the length of a man's hand, handsome orange-red flowers shaped like small hibiscus blossoms— all say *Come, climb me, pluck my leathery fruit.* Some have even suggested that it was no apple which tempted Eve in that proverbial garden, but rather the glittering, jewel-bright seeds of a pomegranate.

Like many things with seductive powers, the pomegranate requires a bit of work once in-hand. You cannot simply bite into it, or slice it at will. First, you must split the outer skin carefully—you will discover, as many pleasure-seekers have before you, that pomegranate juice stains hands and shirts with an unbleachable fuchsia. Second, collect your promised reward using a bowl of cold water, gently prying fingers, and patience. Each fruit contains hundreds of seeds, honey-combed in chamber after chamber, nestled into so many grooves and protected by a film of bitter white pith. Once you have loosened the seeds from their home and discarded both peel and pith, these tiny fruits from the tree of knowledge are yours to enjoy.

In Northwestern India, where my father was born, wild pomegranate bushes grow alongside the tall, slender trunks of cultivated pomegranate trees. This state, Punjab, shares a border with Pakistan and is home to hundreds of farmers, men and women who give this place its title, "Breadbasket of India." For miles as the crow flies outside my father's hometown, the horizon is dominated by orderly rows of crops, broken only occasionally by the brick burner's smoke. Here, pomegranates are considered the gods' fruit, *phal bhavan*, left before Shiva's stone *lingham* or at Durga's marble feet, given as an offering back to the very ones who blessed its budding and growth. If the fruit is sacred, or dangerous (as Persephone, goddess from another land, would attest) that may account for why it tastes so good.

Pomegranates are my favorite fruit, and my father always peeled them for me. He was not a particularly domestic man, so it was the only time I ever saw him wear an apron, seemingly wine-stained and spattered with red, tied delicately around his waist. He bought the fruit by the case and shucked them, like pearl-laden oysters, by the half-dozen. Every autumn, a giant Tupperware container full of seeds sat on a shelf in my parents' refrigerator, rid of pith and ready for my consumption. Each time, my mother would say "You bought too many! No way she will eat them all," but I always did.

Now that he is dead, I find it is my turn to pick my father out of the past, seed by seed, one by one, seemingly endless nooks and crannies. A different kind of harvest.

Most anyone who loves food the way I do owes that love to an enabling relative or family friend: a grandmother who passed down treasured family recipes, a housekeeper who taught young fingers how to measure and pour, a great-aunt who insisted on caviar and tawny port. My own culinary lineage comes from my father, the consummate epicure, and by extension my mother, the cook who made my father's Epicureanism possible. My father is the reason I go to sleep thinking about what I will eat in the morning when I get up; my mother is the reason I read cookbooks for fun.

My father loved food; rather, he was *in* love with it. His unabashed joy in the pleasures of the appetite impacted his every choice, built a thousand little rituals, and couldn't help but show. This passion he passed on to me—not deliberately, the way he taught me my multiplication tables or that I could do anything I set my mind to—but simply by example, without even trying. Because I idolized him when I was young, "monkey see, monkey do" had me training my palate at an early age. I still remember the pride on his face when I agreed to try, and promptly loved, escargot, around age nine. He bragged about this to other dads as if it were a spot on the honor roll. And when it came to my actual school grades, he rewarded all As with a trip out for the pulled-pork barbecue my hometown, Memphis, is famous for. Want to create a foodie child? That's how it's done.

To understand the origins of my own appetite, I had to first understand the origins of my father's. This was something it took me a long while to figure out; I was, as many of us are, naively convinced in my youth that I was a being of my own creation. But when I became an adult, my thoughts finally turned to that blisteringly and embarrassingly simple revelation—my parents were people long before I ever came along. And so I started to ask questions about where the man I had known my whole life had come from.

My father was born poor, poor even by Indian standards, and his family lived with several branches of relatives crowded together in a crumbling second-story apartment in the city of Amritsar, very close to the country's northwest border with Pakistan. He was one of five children, smack dab in the middle between two older sisters and two younger brothers. Though his family lacked materially, they were a loving, affectionate, and pious group—regular trips to temple, regular treats from my grandfather who would willingly spend his last rupee on sweets for his children.

My own father inherited the same generous attitude, but more luck. Utilizing his considerable intelligence, he worked his way up the well-organized school system the British had left behind, earning top grades and scholarships until he was well past the dirty alleyways he had grown up in. He married my mom, came to America, and the two of them worked their asses off to build a comfortable, upper-middle class life that, ironically, would shelter me from any knowledge that my father's childhood had been so radically different from my own.

Mango season may very well have been my father's favorite time of year. He relished the thrill of the catch with the zeal of a mad scientist on the verge of a major discovery: coming home with boxes full of heavy, green-orange fruit, tucking them carefully away into the proper ripening atmosphere of the pantry. Every day, he would harvest the most promising few, upgrading them to a towel-lined basket on the kitchen counter. Then, after dinner, with the sweat beading on his forehead from my mother's homemade *achar* (pickle), the mango monologue began.

"Look at this mango!" he'd exclaim, "Have you ever seen a mango more beautiful than this one?" Holding it in his hand, palm upright, fingering the rich, golden skin, with patches of deep red on either end, smelling it, squeezing it—this was liable to go on for several minutes before he actually cut the thing. But to say that he "cut" is really an injustice. My father could unpack a mango with his eyes closed, knife somehow finding exactly the right spots, working his way deftly around the seed, producing bright, juicy slices of even thickness that I still cannot manage to duplicate.

Once the mango was cut and tasted, it was, of course, time for more speech-making. The flavor, the texture, the perfect ripeness of the fruit. Sometimes he threw in a bit about the bargain price for which he purchased the mango, just for added dramatic effect. Papa was a showman, make no mistake about it. And, for the longest time, I was his favorite audience. My father loved to delight me, to surprise me, and the best way he knew how was with food.

Throughout my elementary school years, I was one of the few kids who were shuttled to the cafeteria for after-school care when the 3:00 bell rang. Even in the early nineties, at St. Mary's Episcopal School in Memphis, Tennessee, only a small number of us had two parents working outside of the home. But on Fridays, I got to sit outside on the sidewalk and wait in the carpool line with all of the "normal" girls, because my dad would leave work early to come pick me up. I remember the anticipation of those afternoons, the white metal column with "M-S" painted on it in black letters, indicating that it was the right place for those of us with corresponding last names—Nishta Mehra, Jenny Maddux, Laura Reddick, Ashley Steinberg—to sit and wait for the on-duty teacher to call our names into a megaphone. My father always arrived in his burgundy Mercedes with the offer of something to eat: hot, buttery movie-theatre popcorn, a stop at Baskin Robbins for Rainbow Sherbet, or, my favorite, a trip to Café Expresso.

Café Expresso was a bakery and restaurant located on the ground floor of the relatively upscale Ridgeway Hotel. With black-and-white tiled floors, beautiful wicker chairs, and fresh flowers on the table, it was exactly the kind of place that made a little girl feel totally sophisticated. I don't think their food was much to speak of, but I wouldn't really know, because it was only for dessert that we always made the trip. For years, their rounded glass pastry case was my personal shrine, cold to the touch. I would stand gazing with awe at the cakes and tortes while my father paid our bill at the nearby register. Silk pie, fruit Bavarian, black forest cake, white chocolate raspberry mousse, all perfectly crafted and adorned with glazes and creams and chocolate shavings. Ideally, a slice or two would be missing from each one, so I could see into the bellies of my favorite confections. Layer upon rich, decadent layer—just my kind of archaeological dig.

Appetite I may have inherited from my father, but any culinary skill I can claim came from my mother. Self-taught, she is a formidable presence in the kitchen with a repertoire that ranges from complex, five-course Indian meals to the Southern classics she learned how to make as the vegetable cook in a University of Oklahoma cafeteria, where my father was an MBA student. Spend ten minutes in my mom's kitchen, and you will quickly discover that she is opinionated, independent, and blazingly competent. And anyone who has spent ten minutes with me in my kitchen knows that I inherited her sharp-eyed, territorial attitude about cooking.

For me, it is a source of pride to spend an entire day cooking from eight to eight, managing to do it all by myself. Though I like to think I am a little bit better than my mom about allowing folks to help me out, I know that my friends would scoff at the notion that I let them do anything but watch. The kitchen the only space in my life where I am conscious of being the alpha.

My cooking habits are about love and control. Here is a little corner of the world where I can make things go right, where my mistakes can simply be thrown in the trash, and my best work delights and literally feeds the people in my life. From my mom, I learned that you do not have to say "I love you" or "You are special to me" if you manage to perfect someone's favorite dish and show up with it at the right time. My mother is uncomfortable telling people flat-out how she feels; I actually believe a part of her finds it uncouth to constantly declare one's emotions. I, on the other hand, have always been a hug-giving, "I love you" dropping open book, known for my proclivity toward emotive talk.

As I get older, though, I appreciate more and more the subtlety of expression that food can bring. While I may feel perfectly comfortable saying out loud how I feel, not everyone feels comfortable hearing it. And the deeper and more nuanced relationships get, the more difficult it can be to truly articulate the layers of feeling within them. Perhaps a blueberry coffee cake seems like the least articulate object in the world, but it helped me communicate to a colleague with a newly dead father so much that in words would have come out inelegantly. I have flirted with people I dare not flirt with outright by dishing out bowls full of spaghetti carbonara, nests of pasta dotted with salty pancetta, the unguent combination of egg and Italian cheese standing in for bodily proximity: sexy, tempting. I compromised only one time on my "no-boxed-mix" rule to recreate the strawberry birthday cake my graduate school colleague remembered her mother baking for her as a little girl. I'll bring you lunch because I know you're too busy to pack your own; I'll send you out the door with leftovers of a dish I noticed you especially liked. I've become one of those women—slightly nutty, just a tinge loud and insistent, who take it personally if you say "no" to dessert.

If people are often like puzzles—and I studied religion and sociology in college, trying to figure them out—all it took was a backwards glance through the story of my own life to realize that the way to unlock most everyone is with an edible key.

My father was a fussy man. Well, "particular" may be a better term. He liked things precisely the way he liked them: no cold sandwiches (he would have dug the recent Panini craze), tea brewed properly and served in a mug (absolutely no Styrofoam), and non-chocolate desserts (preferably with almonds or pecans). His aforementioned favorite pickle, made in batches by my mom, was a triumvirate of cauliflower, carrot, & jalapeno, bathed in a vinegary mix of spices, yellowed like most Indian food by the addition of *haldi*, or turmeric. Orange juice had to be fresh-squeezed only. Salsa had to have enough heat, chips had to have enough heft.

Though he sometimes inconvenienced others with his culinary demands, he was also willing to go to some trouble of his own to satisfy them. We have one especially hilarious photograph of him, bundled up in a ridiculous outfit (replete with 80s-dad Cosby sweater), hovering protectively over a kitchen counter teeming with the jalapeno peppers he had rescued from an impending frost. Each morning, he took the time to practice his very precise method of cooking eggs—scrambled hard, with small wedge of diced red onion, plus salt and lots of freshly ground pepper—which I still crave and make for myself about once a month. But perhaps more than any other food, my father was willing to go the distance for his cucumbers.

Each weekend, he would get up early to drive to the Farmer's Market on Saturday mornings to snag the best cucumbers before they were taken. This was long before buying local produce was hip, so my father easily made friends with the farmers and vendors, chatting them up as he did everyone. You could give my father fifteen minutes with a person—any person—and he could get down to the bottom of what was going on with him or her, their concerns, their ambitions. After he died, I had to go to the Saturday market to let the farmers know he wouldn't be coming anymore; they had bags of their best cucumbers waiting for him to pick up.

My father was superstitious about his cucumbers—I don't know how else to say it, really. During their Southern summer season, he sliced up one or two with every dinner and also for weekend lunch, laid onto the same half-dinner plate with the blue curling pattern on the edge. Somehow he concocted an elaborate ritual, to be performed every time a cucumber was cut and peeled, and he believed that if this ritual were not executed properly and thoroughly, the cucumber in question ran the risk of being be sour and inedible. And seeing as how I never saw my father reject a cucumber after tasting it, nor was I ever served by him a bitter slice, he might have been onto something.

Here's the secret: before peeling the cucumber, slice ½ inch off of the end. Using your knife, make a cross-hatch design into both the exposed edge of the whole cucumber and into the flat side of the cucumber piece. Put the knife down. Pick up both the whole cucumber and the cucumber piece, placing the latter up against its mother cucumber, as if returning it to its original home. Rub the slice against the scored green of the whole cucumber in a back-and-forth motion. Persist until you see white foam forming along the edges where checkerboard flesh meets checkerboard flesh. Only then can you be certain that you have drawn the bitterness out of the cucumber. Discard the end piece, and be sure to slice off another piece at the end, this time only as thick enough as need be to discard the foamy checkerboard. Peel and enjoy your now-guaranteed-sweet summer cucumber.

My father liked his slices dipped into black salt, a slightly sulfurous-smelling mineral salt used almost exclusively in Indian cooking (though there may be some trendy restaurants now also taking part). *Kal namak* does something similar to the Southern-style treatment of watermelon with salt-and-pepper, both enhancing and foiling the sweetness of whatever it accompanies.

My response as a kid was always, "Yuck!" whenever dad accompanied sweet fruit or cucumber with the stinking stuff. Black salt seemed to me to be embarrassingly blatant evidence that we were different, that my life was just an extended version of the "One of these things is not like the other!" game they played on Sesame Street. Other people's dads did not sing Hindi songs while running the bath, did not emerge from said bath dressed in gauzy, white kurta pajamas, did not curse at idiot politicians on TV in another language, and did not insist on dipping cucumber slices in a substance that reeked of hard-boiled egg yolks and looked just like volcanic ash.

Before he died, my parents and I took a trip to India. We did not know he was going to die; it just worked out that way. We arrived late, or rather early, in the wee hours of the morning, and my first taste upon settling into the family apartment was mango. Cool, creamy cubes of mango sliced up for us at three in the morning, Mumbai time, and brought to me on a little tray by my younger, and therefore very deferential, cousins. The fruits' orange was smooth and bright, the color of a marigold with rounded and slippery edges. These, the coveted Alphonso mangoes, king of all fruit, are very, very difficult to come by in America; I had never eaten one before. When it touched my lips, it completely obliterated what I had heretofore defined as the taste, "mango." My brain puzzled—I was twenty-three years old, had eaten plenty of mangos in my life (and listened to my dad rave rapturously about them for years), but there was no match in my food file for the taste I was experiencing. I reached for another bite: sweet, sorbet-smooth, perfect.

Conversation hummed around me, gentle, late-night, long anticipated. The velvety feeling in my mouth was joy, food joy becoming family joy, there I was in India, place that I am somehow from, and the mangoes tasted like magic and I had three weeks of this ahead of me, three weeks of discovering all the things that I never knew I never knew.

"Now this," I said to my father as I pointed down into my bowl, "This is a mango worth making a speech over." My parents and I laughed at our inside joke.

India taught me why my father loved a buffet. I ought to have figured it out much sooner, but it took visiting his hometown, seeing where he literally came from, to realize that it was his younger self, little Subhash, who had once scraped coins together for a single hot *jalebi* from the man who fried them in a giant wok of oil down the street from my father's childhood home, that drew adult Subhash, and his family with him, to buffet after buffet. After all, a buffet is the ultimate demonstration of choice and infinite possibility. What could be more American than that? The buffet says—*Come eat at our communal table; you made it, you are one of us*. Each visit was a victory for little Subhash, who could finally have as much as he wanted, and could eat without being rushed.

My mother tells stories about epic, three-hour Pizza Hut visits with my dad, before I was born; he would wait for new pizzas to come out, taking one or two slices from the fresh, hot pie, then wait for another to arrive. I experienced firsthand my father's proclivity towards long stays at the buffet table. Back when Shoney's still dotted the landscape below the Mason-Dixon line, family trips there for the breakfast buffet were a fairly regular occurrence. There my father had *two* women waiting on him to finish, but he still never bothered to rush. My mother and I played a lot of games of tic-tac-toe in crayon on the back of my kids' menu as a result. As a teenager, I even spent one New Year's Eve at Memphis' last Shoney's, dancing in the empty aisles with my mother and friends to Marvin Gaye while my father waited for fresh biscuits to come out of the restaurant oven.

For most of my young life, my father's employer was a local chain of restaurants called Pancho's, arguably the best option for Tex-Mex food in Memphis, at least while I was growing up. Looking back, it's hard to know whether it was the kind of place that I would go now myself, as a grownup. I can't accurately assess what kind of clientele it served, or how much anything cost. I will also admit to having become something of a food snob these last few years, so I wonder if I would turn my nose up at all kinds of things I enjoyed as a kid. Sometimes the things we try to revisit don't hold water anymore.

Back then, though, to me Pancho's was the coolest. We went to dinner there about once a week, and because my father was a "big boss," it was something of a big deal when we showed up. Dad was the Vice-President of Manufacturing and Shipping, which meant that he managed the plant which produced the restaurant's chips, dips, tamales, and sauces. I remember memorizing his title off of his business card that I could say it, impressively, because even then I was conscious that he worked in a plant in a not-very-glamorous part of town, near the airport, where all of the packing and shipping and manufacturing tends to happen.

I went to work with him on several occasions—he had a fancy office with a big green chair and all kinds of fun things on his desk.

He would give me a big, print-out calculator and old invoices or a legal pad & pen so I could conjure up an imaginary business and busy myself making calculations, drawing up figures, printing out receipts. Employees would come in and out of his office during the day, always pausing to greet or tease me. A polite child who heard again and again, "You're so mature for your age!," I remember feeling shy but wanting to do my father proud and earn him credit in their eyes.

Though I idolized my dad like nearly all young kids do, I believe I read correctly the respect and general affection with which his employees treated him. Many of the older black women who worked in the plant sent Dad home at Christmas with greens, ham, and homemade pies. For about two months in elementary school, I shared a shower with my parents because *my* shower (which doubled as the guest-bedroom shower) and the bedroom to which it was attached were occupied by an employee of my father's. He was recently divorced and had no place to go. He lived like a kind of ghost in our house: occasionally appearing at the kitchen table or on the staircase. I sensed that his presence made my mother uncomfortable, but if there had been an argument about it, my father had won.

Though the experience felt awkward at the time, its larger meaning stuck with me. And in the way that most of us come to examine our childhoods with ever more powerful lenses, at some point I realized just what my father had done, that this had been an extraordinary act. That it was, in fact, something that most people wouldn't be willing to do, an idea that would never even occur to them.

When I was a freshman in high school, a stress test led to the discovery of serious blockage in my father's three major arteries. Epicureanism, never tempered by exercise, comes with a high price. The second time I ever saw him cry was in a hospital room, as he was being prepped for triple-bypass surgery. His was a long hospital

stay; I became accustomed to winding through corridors and keeping phone numbers in my purse at all times, sitting in the cafeteria with my journal and trying not to be scared. He came out of
recovery much skinnier, with a Frankenstein scar running down
his left leg. Unblocking his arteries unblocked something else; he
became a far more emotional man from then on, crying easily, an
unexpected change. For my part, I never forgot the units of blood
he had received in the hospital; they wouldn't allow me to bank for
him, I was too young. Barring a few dozen months off for tattoos
and travel, I have donated whole blood or platelets regularly since
the day I turned seventeen.

Once recuperated, my father found himself laid off from his
executive-level job at Pancho's. Though even I knew at the time
that he had been unfairly, not to mention illegally treated by his
employer, I believe that the shame of being without a job was more
than enough to quell any desire on my parents' part to seek retribu-
tion. "That's an American thing," they said. Apparently the Indian
way is to suffer in silence.

My father spent a year-and-a-half in unemployment.
Unemployment, as if it were a place, with geographic features and
a landscape. It was a domain for him alone; he was forced there,
on exile. My mother, now the sole bread-winner in our household,
was working harder than ever, busy with work and busy replacing
things in our refrigerator where butter substitute and two-percent-
milk cheese became the norm. She was the one who had broken the
news to me, and her telling of it communicated implicitly that my
parents didn't want me to act like anything was wrong. My duty
in all of this was to not make a fuss, not ask for a lot of things, and
work hard in school—school where I had, thank goodness, received
a half-tuition scholarship to help keep us afloat.

My parents did an incredible job of rocking the boat so mini-
mally that I was spared most of the severely wounding impact these
changes were having. I *do* remember seeing my father dressed in the
mornings, readying his briefcase with papers for job interviews from
which he always came back unsuccessful. Mom told me later that he

kept hearing one of two lines: "You're overqualified," or, said without saying it, "Too old." Watching him was awful, the beginnings of parent-child reversal, where all of a sudden you are the one who can't fix it, can't make it go away. Here is your father, vulnerable, humiliated, and you want to say everything to him, tell him that you are sorry, but you are so afraid that you'll only make it worse.

In what turned out to be the last picture ever taken of my father, he is sitting in my uncle's marble-floored apartment in Mumbai, smiling from his seat on the plush, gold-embroidered couch. On the table in front of him is a plate with a *malpura*, a sweet pancake traditionally eaten in India during the rainy monsoon season. Three days before we left Mumbai, the rain began falling in sheets, and my father had to commemorate the occasion, like he commemorated everything else, with food.

It's not an overstatement to say that the picture represents almost everything you need to know about him. He's smiling the sweet, easy, generous smile that came naturally to him. He is looking out at the camera, holding a phone in one hand, since he's in the middle of calling everyone we're related to in Bombay (a small army's worth of people) and saying goodbye. His shirt is short-sleeved and collared, American style, pale yellow with horizontal bands of white flocked with light blue. For pants he wears the traditional Indian *kurta* pajama bottoms, thin, gauzy, loose, and drawstring. His reading glasses sit on the table in front of him.

It took me years, but I finally learned to like, and then love the taste of Scotch. The whole endeavor was a deliberate project that originated with the whisky collection my father left behind. I took the drink as a filial obligation, another one of those daughter-as-son moments that happen to us who are only children. With no one else to fill the role, we inherit the neckties and the funeral decisions, the taking care of mom, the eulogy writing, the necessary phone calls. I'm not sure what he would think now that I've worked my way through his old collection, and added favorite bottles of my own; probably equal parts delighted and mortified, the way he was when I smuggled him a Cuban cigar from my college trip to Amsterdam, the single, deliberately law-breaking act of my life.

When someone dies, they take things with them: the restaurant you cannot bear to go to without him, the ability for your child to ever know his grandfather, the singing voice you wish you had hours of recorded. But at the same time, the dead leave ties behind. My father left his favorite foods, his meticulous eating habits, and quirky preferences. I imagine him visiting my kitchen from wherever he has gone and daring me, cajoling me to cook a feast worthy of him. He will never show up to eat it, so I feed other mouths in his stead.

Biscuits he would drool over? I can make them, and with lard I rendered myself. The authentic Indian dishes he craved? I grind my own spices to go in them. You name it, I can make it, or if I can't, I will teach myself how. In the whipping of a meringue or pressing of a crust for a tart, I build my own rituals, enact the missing of him in edible form, over and over and over. The kitchen is where I am happiest, most creative, free. I ache for my father and I honor my mother. I cook.

7

History of Us

*This is a love story that begins with my parents
and ends with my son.*

It was universally accepted that, whoever you married, you would fall in love with; we didn't question it." That was the reality in which my mother was raised; not that she would choose a husband, but that one would be chosen for her, and she would automatically love him. Funny, then, that the classic Hindi movies my mom's generation grew up watching are full of sweeping, romantic, ridiculous and grand love—passionate pleas from lovesick men, ballads from doe-eyed ladies singing in the highest possible register. Perhaps they served as a kind of cultural antidote to the business of marriages arranged, by the old, for the young.

We, each of us, rehearse for parts all our lives long: husband, wife, mother, father. And even if we don't quite fit, even if we come to resent the part, we still reference the measure, feel some familiarity in what we've known we were going to do all along. After all, it isn't only in arranged-marriage cultures that folks fall in love through the power of suggestion. Here in America we are raised to think that we will meet someone and fall in love, and so we do, for the most part. Even dealing with the most unpleasant circumstances in family and marriage *that we could see coming* can prove to be heartening, because our willing sacrifice is an indication that we're doing this "right." It's when the script suddenly calls for roles we never understudied for (widow) or ever saw performed (lesbian daughter) that those comforting cultural norms start to work against us.

This is how my parents met: twice before their wedding day.

They were married on December 8, 1967. My mom was twenty, my dad was twenty-five.

My mother always said, "I got married, had sex, and then fell in love. Please do it in some order other than that."

The first time my parents met, my mother wasn't paying close attention. Traveling with her father, step-mother, and other relatives, she had been told that they were stopping at a house to check out a potential groom for my mother's aunt, who was close to her in age and unmarried. The truth, of course, was that the visit was for the sake of my mother's own future. In arranged marriage communities, gossip and "prospects" are constantly batted back-and-forth, and this was how her family had heard of a young man, Subhash, who was handsome, well-educated, and ambitious; they thought their Veena might impress him with her matching qualities.

I assume that my mom was kept in the dark because her family thought that she would act more natural and be less self-conscious if she were unaware that the sole purpose of this visit was for her inspection. But, the secrecy backfired. Confused and bored by the niceties of the visit, she excused herself out to the garden to have a look around: a sequence of events totally consistent with the person she is today. Then, as if in a scripted comedy, everyone else got up and followed her outside.

In her retelling of this story, my mother stops to take a sip of her coffee, then holds the mug out in front of her, gesticulating as she says, "I thought, 'What the heck is going on?'" She pauses.

"Well, I wouldn't have said it *quite* like that back then, but I knew something was up."

After my parents' first, haphazard meeting, they asked my mom, "How do you like that boy?"

"What do you mean, how do I like him? For my cousin?"

"No, for you. He was looking at you, and he's interested."

Though my mother hadn't paid much attention the first time around, my father had. A beautiful woman, well-educated, working towards her Masters—she met two of his highest marks; if only he had known what an amazing cook she would turn out to be, he would have married her on the spot.

But he needed to hear her speak English; he wanted to ask her himself if she had any objections to traveling outside India, to England or to America. And so a second meeting was arranged, at a Kwality [sic] Restaurant, a chain which at the time dotted the hotels of larger cities in India and featured an assortment of Hindu-friendly Continental fare, as interpreted by Indian chefs: vegetable soufflés, soups, crepes. My mother and father sat at one table, with my father's friend as chaperone, and both sets of parents sat far across the room at another table, watching. Not exactly the ideal set-up for romance.

But my mother had gone to a co-ed college; she was not afraid of talking to boys. "I was one of the boldest girls in my class. I had friends who were boys." She did not sit like a timid mouse; she didn't just smile demurely and agree. My father, for his part, was the product of two older sisters and was used to being around strong women. Plus, as it turned out, my mom spoke excellent English and had no qualms about leaving the country, checking off my father's two other criteria. I remember him telling me that he fell for her that day; for her part, cynical and hardened as she is now, she insists the same: "Your father was cute."

He was cute, he was a gentleman, and he was sold. His family gave *takka* soon after that meeting. *Takka* is a gift that usually consists of money and jewelry, given as a "hold" or a promise on the girl. A statement of intention, with some weight. A claim. A down payment, if you will. This seems strange until one thinks of the Western custom of an engagement ring, which is supposed to cost the equivalent of two months of a man's salary.

This is where it gets tricky. Where I can rely only on my mother's telling, and guess what in that telling is skewed, and what is true. This is where my grandfather plays the bad guy.

My mother was born in 1947, just over a month before India gained its independence. Due to the violence that took place over the Partition of northern states, my mom's family had to move from Kashmir, her birthplace, to the state of Utter Pradesh, where she grew up. Her mother died when she was two years old, having only just given birth to a son, my uncle Mohan. My grandfather remarried fairly quickly, a woman my mother has no recollection of, and divorce took place almost as quickly. He then courted a number of women before settling on my step-grandmother. My mother remembers, or somehow knows, that he had a thing for fair-skinned nurses, fair-skinned like him, like my mother. There was another woman, one I think my mother has always wished he had chosen, tall, the principal of a nearby school, who came and watched my mother on the playground as a little girl. "That's the woman your father almost married," someone told her. Instead he chose her, my *Nani*, though I was never raised to call her that or think of her as my grandmother. Eleven years younger than my grandfather and from a wealthy family, she soon bore two children of her own, a son first and then a daughter.

My step-grandmother is a strange woman. She has a kind of child-like quality, frozen in her capabilities in a way that makes sense for a spoiled girl who was never very smart and who only ever expected to be married off and bred anyway. She is a woman who is not much in touch with reality, who is too much of a child herself to have been a very good parent. Maybe it didn't occur to her that playing favorites would be hurtful to her stepchildren, still so young and in need of affirmation from a mother of some kind. Perhaps she did not care.

While their stepmother ignored them and indulged their new half-siblings, my mother and her brother became a unit, solid, of one mind, just as in a fairy tale, except no one came to rescue them. They begged books from every nearby house, reading anything they could get their hands on, bothering servants, climbing trees. My mother, who has always had a taste for the sour, stole lemons and limes from neighbors' trees. My uncle, disobedient, rebellious, and angry, just plain stole. He was punished in the way boys often are, beaten and called names by his father—intelligent as my grandfather is, it seems not to have occurred to him that his child might simply be thirsting for attention, might want affection, might shamefully blame himself for his own mother's death.

Their "new mother" devoted her time and attention to her son, following him around the house with cups of milk, "Drink, *beta*, drink." Her smothering had the opposite, if logical effect—her biological son moved about as far away from India as he possibly could— for all of his adult life he has lived in Australia.

Growing up, I never heard my mother speak much about her father, except to scoff or blame: that he had married the awful woman, that he had not interfered or intervened. I know that at some point my mother must have adored and idolized her father, felt love for him and loved by him, that she was probably his favorite, the smartest, the most capable, born an adult, the most like him. I know this because she could not have become so angry with him later if she did not love him so much as a child. I understand how these things work, myself.

You cannot pull the wool over my mother's eyes, at least not for very long. She is deeply skeptical, cynical even, and unsentimental in ways that troubled my Pollyanna-self as a child. While not quite a stereotypical "Tiger Mom," she *was* a fierce boundary maven of house rules and expectations, drawing up behavior contracts for me to sign and never hesitating to say "no" when an event I requested permission to attend was outside her acceptable parameters. Please see: missing my best friend's graduation party because my Algebra II exam was the next day, my tenth grade weekend night curfew of 10:30 p.m., and the fact that during summer vacations as an elementary student, Mom would have me choose topics from the encyclopedia (I remember being particularly proud of my piece about the "tundra") and turn in reports on them by the end of each week.

At the same time, I know of no mother more doting than my own, more prone to spoil with favorite foods, more beloved by my entire group of friends, more committed to my personhood thriving in the world. When your mother is tough to please and not prone to brag or be effusive and does not hesitate to tell you *exactly* what she thinks when asked (whether the answer is to your liking or not), you know her praise and compliments are genuine, and they go quite a long way. Of all the "aunties" in the group of Indian immigrants in which I was raised, my mom (Veena Aunty) was the one my fellow first-generation kids went to when they needed straight talk about sex or teenager-appropriate advice. She is an always candid, politically astute, slightly misanthropic ball of contradictions, this mother of mine.

My mom is the eldest child in her family, and a stereotypical one at that: duty bound, responsible. As an adult, I don't think she has ever once slacked off or once done something she *wanted* to do instead of something she thought she *ought* to do. And yet she tells me stories of herself as a little girl, how she loved to dance, would make up her own choreography to whatever music was playing, that she would become so absorbed in un-self-conscious joy that her family would put on Hindi film songs just to watch her twirl. How could that child have become my mother?

A few years after I started teaching, I brought my mother to school with me for a day to visit. She sat in my classroom and participated with my sixth graders, sitting in a desk, in a circle of desks, as we went around the circle taking turns reading aloud from the chapter of a book. She watched me with my students, who were fascinated by her presence—*Mrs.* Mehra, the mother of the *Ms.* Mehra they knew—and at the end of the day, she paid me the compliment of my life. "I wish I could go back and have you as my English teacher," she said. "I would have loved school a lot more."

Where we start and finish, how much of our past selves remain— these are questions on my almost-thirty-year-old mind, and it is my mother about whom I wonder the most. She is the surviving half of my parents' original pair, the one who has been left behind to deal with the mess that results when things don't go according to plan. So to catch a glimpse of her as a little girl, impossibly young, with crushes on movie stars and a proclivity to dance, would be to know her before life had had as much of a chance to make its mark, to disappoint, scare, and sadden her.

Though she was already betrothed to my father, my mom was taken to meet another family and again put up for inspection. "It's like a cattle show," she gripes in recollection. "You sit there and they gawk at you." The potential mate in question was twenty years my mom's elder, a major in the Armed Forces, and everything my mom did not want in a husband. On principle, she refused to marry a man whose education didn't match hers, and he hadn't gone to college. Plus, she didn't like the way his family looked at her.

Her parents insisted anyway. Though my father was busy sending her letters and presents (a watch, a book—the title of which I desperately wish she could remember), my mother was forced to go and meet the major when his train passed through their town. Her stepmother prepared a *tiffin* canister with food, and took my mother to deliver it. "He wanted me to sit next to him, he kept trying to touch me. It was awful, so degrading. I thought 'Why is my father doing this to me? The other family has already given *takka*.'"

But the major's family was wealthier; they had a house, more status. They, too, gave *takka*, unaware that my father was even in the picture. And my father had no idea that any of this was going on. My mother was furious, and *crack*, the rift between her and her father was born. My grandfather brought in her favorite teachers from school, asked them to talk to her, convince her to do what he wanted. He offered to cancel both "engagements" and start over, find her a new husband. "I'd like to say I was being all independent, insisting that I marry your father, but it was just so awful, the whole process. I didn't understand why my father was doing this to me. I thought I was playing by the rules."

In a strange twist of fate, it was my step-grandmother who intervened and convinced my grandfather to send back the army family's *takka*, to marry my mother to my father. Who knows what possessed her to take my mother's side for the first (and last) time? I suspect it was my father, young Subhash, who had already charmed my step-grandmother; she has always had a soft spot for him.

And so, my parents were married on a cold December morning, the actual wedding ceremony taking place at 4:00 am, because that's when the Hindu priests' astrological calculations determined that the marriage should take place. In black and white pictures, my parents sit next to each other, covered with the same blanket, hands wrapped symbolically together, looking very handsome, very young, and completely terrified. Friends and family arrived for a celebratory breakfast after the ceremony was done.

My father's father, a kindly, generous man whose business schemes mostly failed but whose sense of humor and optimism never dimmed, took a real shine to my mother. The day of my parents' wedding, *Dadaji* slipped a ring into my mother's hand, a ring that had belonged to his late wife, gold and inlaid with enamel, a tall, colorful piece. Though her relationship with her *own* father was never the same, she has worn that ring faithfully ever since.

These are the things I know about my maternal grandfather:

1. He was born in 1921.
2. He made his living as a labor lawyer for a textile mill (one of many that resulted from Gandhi's "khadi" movement).
3. He insisted that my mother receive as good of an education as her brother.
4. He has an abiding love for British literature, which my mother and I both inherited.
5. He has beautiful penmanship, which neither my mother nor I inherited.
6. I look like him.

My *Nanaji* lived right in the thick of things; he was an adult at the time of Partition and Independence, a man, a lawyer, paid to think about ideals and justice and freedom and how they should be materialized in the world. So I can't help but wonder at the drama of it all, guess about the stories that surely lie behind his choice of a wife, her craziness, and my mother's grief and anger. But the truth is that the truth doesn't matter. What we perceive is what we carry with us; it becomes our truth, and we hold onto it like a flag. As a student of non-fiction, I know all too well that it doesn't matter much what the "real story" is about my mom's childhood, or the divide between her and her father. It's what she remembers that makes her reality, that made her clear about what kind of parent she did *not* want to be, that has informed nearly every one of her actions since.

No shortage of irony here: my mother's father, with whom she barely has a relationship (and with whom I, by extension, feel little connection) is still living. My father, who rescued my mother from her joyless nuclear family and with whom I would give anything to have a hundred more conversations, has been dead for these half-a-dozen years.

After their wedding, my parents took a honeymoon in the Himalayas, then were forced to live apart for a few months due to financial constraints: my father working, my mother staying with his family (a less-than-ideal arrangement). Eventually, they were able to rent a small house in Bombay with citrus trees in the courtyard, my father working a good job as an electrical engineer for a company that sent a very rare private car to his flat every morning, and my mom working (also very rare in those days), teaching at a little Montessori school within walking distance from their house.

But America had always been the objective, and so they made the necessary sacrifices to get themselves here. Again, they could not afford to come together. He didn't ask her to, but she sold the gold jewelry and silver tea set from her dowry to buy my father's plane ticket. My parents, the O. Henry short story protagonists: her long, dark hair, his handsome doe eyes.

In the fall of 1969, just a year and a half after they were married, my father enrolled in graduate courses at the University of Oklahoma in Norman. From India to Oklahoma in one fell swoop, flying into the crucible of American history, the melting pot really just getting started, with Congress lifting immigration quotas, making it a bit easier for students like my father to get visas and scholarships.

My mom was able to join my father in 1970; he had to borrow three thousand dollars from a friend and deposit it into his own bank account to prove to the immigration authorities that he would be able to support his wife, should they allow her to come to the United States. For her part, she visited countless doctors for chest x-rays to prove she did not carry tuberculosis (the disease that had killed her mother) and took laxatives so the health of her bowels could be verified: a different kind of cattle show. Thusly inspected, my mother passed all of the various tests and flew to America on borrowed funds, leaving her father's house for the very last time.

They lived on-campus in an apartment for married students in graduate hosing. My mother wasn't able to legally work during the first year, so while my father went to his classes, she was alone. Other student's wives would offer her rides to the grocery store or help her navigate the Laundromat, but you can be alone in America in a way that never would be possible in India. There is more space, there are less bodies, and a different conception of privacy. Her habits developed then; America was her adulthood, in a sense, she was only twenty-one. There she was, finally someplace else, the long-sought a room of one's own. A life of her own choosing, albeit with adjustments: "I just never could get over that you had to go buy your own groceries, put them on the shelf, cook your own food, wash dishes. You find yourself at the bottom of the totem pole. What kind of life is that?"

They were so poor that the only luxury they could afford was a radio, which is how my mother fell in love with Western music. She had never been exposed to any of it before, though some of the names were familiar to her from newspapers and magazines. "I had heard of The Beatles, The Rolling Stones, but I had never heard them sing. I took to it right away." Keeping a pen and paper nearby, she would write down the names of artists and songs, guessing at some spellings, learning her favorites. We still have a stack of the first LPs she bought, some years later, when they could afford a fancy player in a towering case. Simon & Garfunkel, America, The Eagles, Billy Joel, Chicago, Olivia Newton-John. I grew up listening to all of it, listening to the radio just like her, with new tape technology that allowed me to capture what I was hearing, play it again. My brain is full of reels and snarls of music—my partner Jill calls me "the jukebox"—there is always a song in my head. I know the soundtrack of the generation that predates me because my mother sat alone in that tiny apartment listening to music before the American government would let her work.

This is how you write your parents' love story: you look at a lot of photographs.

When you look, you see what a knockout my mother was—there is a kind of resonance with Cher: long, dark hair and a beautiful size 6 body, at once so young and flawless and yet so womanly. My dad was handsome, though not in an intimidating way, and carried his baldness well, like a mark of sophistication. He was rounder in his younger years, thanks to my mom's good cooking and his voracious appetite: this was before the type II diabetes & heart disease were discovered. It seems impossible that they could have ever been so young, picnicking by the Mississippi river and laughing into the camera, going on my dad's business trips to Las Vegas, road tripping with friends to Texas.

As a young couple, my parents worked together at a restaurant called Pancho's, in Memphis. He was the manager, and she was a bartender. I really love the fact that my India-born mother used to tend bar in a Tex-Mex restaurant in the deep South. This stuff only happens in America; you can't write it any better. She was beautiful, and she brought home plenty of tips.

Underneath the surface, though, if you know the story, you can see a tight layer of pain. My parents spent those years trying, unsuccessfully, to have a baby. Three others before me had failed to come into the world; none of the siblings who preceded me in utero had made it past their fifth month of pre-life. Following these miscarriages, my parents spent two years and several thousands of dollars on fertility treatments from the Emory Clinic in Atlanta, my mother taking the forty-five minute flight from Memphis once a month for doctors to inject her with this and that and then send her back home. None of it worked. Exhausted and depressed, in December of 1981, my parents gave up the treatments.

I did not fully understand what this meant until I had to wait for my own child. Adoption is not the same context as infertility, but occupying the space of without-a-baby comes with similar textures, I think. Every pregnant woman at the grocery store is like a punch in the gut; your friends have babies and you are happy for them, but you hurt so much. You wonder how long you will have to wait.

In February of 1982, I was conceived, and in November of that same year, I was born.

This is the number of children my parents had: one, me.

Both of my parents grew up meatless in India—at that time, no proper Hindus would dare do otherwise—but started eating meat when they came to America. Dad gave into beef right away; apparently one of his fellow Indian graduate students convinced him, "Look, this is not Lord Krishna's cow, it's okay." My mom, on the other hand, ate beef for only one month of her life, the eighth month she was pregnant with me. At the time, my father was working as a regional manager for Wendy's, and one day my mother called him craving a hamburger.

"How do you know you want a hamburger when you've never even had one?" my father asked. Why he bothered asking is a mystery to me, as I should think one would not wish to trifle with any woman, let alone my mother, when she is eight months pregnant. In any case, Mom had indeed pinpointed the exact location of her body's desire, and Dad kept the hamburgers coming all month. (This should explain a lot about my own beef-eating habits, most notably the compulsion I feel to have a really good cheeseburger every four to six weeks.) All in all, my mother gained forty pounds in the nine months she carried me, forty pounds to insulate and incubate a successful pregnancy.

When she was first found out she was pregnant with me, my mother made a bargain with God. The deal was this: if I made it safely to term, if I were born the healthy, bouncing thing she had prayed to Shiva for, had tried for throughout the fifteen years of her marriage, she would give up meat entirely. And after I spent a successful year on this earth, she did. She never stopped cooking it for my dad or for me and she hardly ever talked about why she had chosen to give it up, since most people always assumed it was an Indian-woman-thing. But the truth is that my mom is a vegetarian because she is relentless. And because she never breaks a promise, not even when she doubts the existence of the being to whom it was made.

This is what my childhood was like: happy.

There are many pieces of American kitsch that the immigrant adopts with guileless joy, and in my house growing up, breakfast at Waffle House was a prime example. My parents' outsider status made the great American diner something of a novelty; they seemed happy to adopt the traditions of the landscape where they had landed, the American South. When you live in a country that refers to everything about your home culture as "exotic," there's a hidden irony in turning the tables. Plus, I think that my parents' memories of being young and poor in Norman, Oklahoma—an experience which, after surviving, they became nostalgic for—fed the tradition. Whatever the reasons, we were the only family I know who went to Waffle House on special occasions like birthdays and anniversaries. While other kids squirmed through fancy meals with unpronounceable food, I learned to order pecan waffles and to ask for my hash browns scattered, smothered, and well-done.

We were also regulars at a restaurant called Buntyn's, a good, ole-fashioned, blue-plate-special kind of place, family-run and with waitresses who called you "Hun" and meant it. Our waitress was Sandy and we only went to Buntyn's on days that she worked. We sat in the non-smoking section in the back and I ordered the meat of the day (meatloaf, fried chicken, spaghetti) with mashed potatoes—no gravy—and a dinner salad with more ranch dressing on it than vegetables. One of the walls of the back room had been decorated with cheap 8x10 portraits of the American presidents, arranged in chronological order from Washington to Clinton (when we were last there). I occupied myself by memorizing their names while my parents chatted with Sandy and dug into dessert—peach cobbler a la mode, their favorite.

My family also took a lot of road trips. There's nothing more quintessentially more American than the inefficient vacation, the romance of the open road. We had the means to, but we did not go on glamorous, cosmopolitan trips involving four-star hotels and

concierge; because my parents were as unfamiliar with the landscape
of this country as I was, they set out to explore it and simultaneously
show it to me. Sometimes just to a cabin in a mountain-y place—
central Arkansas, eastern Tennessee—where we would play cards
and read books, go for hikes and drink tea in the afternoons, other
times on epic jags, like our infamous drive from Memphis to Niagara
Falls, with stops at Lincoln's birthplace in Kentucky and the Henry
Ford museum in Michigan. Two staples of Mehra family vacation
photos: a picture of me avoiding having my picture taken, fed up
with my father's incessant urge to document every, little thing, and
a picture of my father napping somewhere ridiculous—on a park
bench, next to a monument, on display at the zoo as if he were one
of the featured animals.

This was our last vacation together: three weeks in India.

A memory: we are killing time during the hottest part of the
afternoon, waiting until it cools a bit to ride in a taxi to the border
where India meets Pakistan. We are staying in two hotel rooms here
in Amritsar, a welcome oasis of comfort for my spoiled, western self:
central air conditioning! American-style toilets and showers! I don't
have to share my bed with anyone! Funny, though I have my own
room for the first time in weeks, I find myself sitting on the bed
in my parents' room, knees up to my chest, writing postcards. My
dad is flipping channels on the bed next to me. He comes across an
old black-and-white movie and puts down the remote. "Hey Veena,
look!" My mother turns away from her ironing.

The movie is in Punjabi, of which I understand very little, though
I can distinguish it from Hindi when I hear it spoken. But this is
not the kind of movie that requires an extensive vocabulary anyway.
From what I can tell, it's one of those good old-fashioned screwball
comedies, full of mistaken identities and haphazard plots to get the
girl. It's goofy and simple but my parents are having so much fun

watching this film in their old language that soon they are practically rolling on the floor. My mom does this thing when she laughs, and I mean *really* laughs—she starts clicking her tongue and slapping her right hand on her thigh, as if she just can't believe anything could be so funny, that it's almost a shame. And since she rarely laughs that fully, her laughter becomes contagious, so soon my father is "hee heeing" and tearing up and shaking the bed next to me, breathing hard in between fits of laughter.

So of course, I'm laughing, too, watching the silly actor whose eyes bulge wide every time he gets hit on the head with something (a motif in this film), but mostly watching my parents laughing and laughing myself out of disbelief. I can't remember the last time I heard them laugh together like this, simultaneously and unabashedly. And now here I am, giggling over a movie in a language I don't understand, blurring the ink on the postcards in my lap, shaking my head at my parents in disbelief, and unable to articulate exactly why I am feeling joy beyond measure.

Mexican food was always the cuisine of choice for the three of us. We are, after all, the same family that ate Mexican food non-stop for a week straight, breakfast, lunch, and dinner, when my father took us to Texas ten years ago on a "research trip" as part of his job with Pancho's. A lovely trip, fortuitously scheduled in my tenth or eleventh year of life, back when I was still rapturously in love with both of my parents and free of adolescent angst. While my father did precipitate some icy stretches in the car by getting us lost with his notoriously bad sense of direction, all in all that trip is among my fondest food and family memories (you are, I'm sure, starting to see how the two are often one in my world). I ate my first breakfast tacos on that trip, my first chorizo. While my father took tours of restaurant kitchens, Mama and I people-watched. All three of us lusted after authentic tortillas being pressed and griddled before our eyes.

We did other things, too, visiting the Alamo in San Antonio, the Space Museum in Houston, The Sixth Floor Museum in Dallas. I look back at our photos and feel a little thrill, recognizing the park in downtown Houston, city I now call home. And it's one of my favorite (and true) family stories, the fact that we drove home from our Texas trip and decided to cook Mexican food for dinner that night.

Following that trip, each Mehra family member perfected his or her respective dinner contributions, and between my mother's margaritas, my guacamole, and my father's painstakingly-perfected, vegetarian-so-my-mom-could-eat-them, but-you-wouldn't-believe-there-isn't-any-lard-in-these refried beans, we could conjure up a better feast at home than anywhere you could go in Memphis. After my dad died, mom found a container full of those beans of his in the freezer, insisted that I take them back to graduate school with me. I ate them on the floor of my little apartment, scooping them out with the freshest tortillas I could find, crying into the empty, re-purposed plastic container that had once held generic "whipped topping," my mom's strange vice. She, these many years later, is still attempting to recreate Dad's magical, secret beans; I have taken to attempting my own version, but I don't think either one of us wants to get them right. Sometimes it means more when things are lost.

This is how long my parents had been married on the day my father died: thirty-eight years, seven months, and fourteen days.

He was sixty-four. My mother was fifty-nine. I was twenty-three.

Not long after my father's death, our close group of friends (known as the Arkansas Group) presented us with a lovely, half-filled scrapbook with pages contributed by them and other community friends.

One of the more tangible gifts our community offered us in the wake of my father's death, the album features a wonderful, full-smiling picture of my father on the front, dressed up for the last wedding he went to: red tie, blue-gray suit jacket, handsome white beard. Included inside are some pretty bottom-of-the-barrel pictures; not surprising, since my father was almost always the one behind the camera. But if the visuals aren't terribly flattering, the accompanying words go beyond affirming. The testimony inside that book assures me that either everyone else is also engaged in the project of white-washing my father after his death, or he really was a pretty fantastic guy.

My mother has, as I recently discovered, filled the rest of the book with pictures from our own collection and captions written in her (sadly inherited by me) non-artistic handwriting. There are many I don't remember seeing before, young photos of them in India, in Biloxi, Mississippi, or Norman, Oklahoma. One in particular strikes me—my mom's arms are draped around my father's neck and shoulders like a human scarf, in that sweet, clingy way high school girls pose with their boyfriends. She looks so *happy*; so young in a way it's hard to imagine her being.

A few pages later, familiar pictures, ones I took myself. Every year, like a good North Indian woman, my mother would fast all day for the long life of her husband. *Karva Chauth*, as the occasion is known, means one thing when you're sitting at home and can nap all day long, waiting for servants to prepare your fast-breaking meal. But my mom did hers on long days of work and mothering, every year without fail. It was always my job to stand outside at the end of the day and wait for the moon to show its face, indicating that my mother could eat again.

Somewhat more unusually, it was my father who cooked my mother's evening *Karva Chauth* meal. He loved doing it. Like many things he did, he made the meal more elaborate and ritualized than it needed to be. He liked to make a fuss out of things, and then take pictures of the fuss. So the effort that went into his work has been documented: though my mother cooked nearly every other meal in our house, my father learned how to make her favorite *daal* (lentil stew) for the occasion, and rice to go along with it. He would grate cucumber into cool yogurt *raita*, but instead of mixing in the spices, he would sprinkle them carefully on top to spell "LOVE VEENA." As if that weren't enough, Papa also assembled a raw vegetable medley on my mother's octagonal, pink-pattern-ed platter (the pattern is scandalously called "Mary Jane," which my mother loves to tell people), replete with radish roses and a green-bell-pepper half centerpiece with "VEENA" carved into it.

In this latest scrapbook, underneath the pictures which document these occasions, my mother has written "All that fasting did not help! Fate can be cruel indeed!"

This is when my son, Shiv, was born: five days before the sixth anniversary of my father's death.

Two ultrasounds told us that he would be a girl, but—he shares his initials (SCM) with his late grandfather.

My father was most definitely a rajah in his past life. Well-suited to being pampered and spoiled, at least when it came to the comforts of domestic life. He liked his baths long, his tea piping hot, and his food made fresh to order. He was, as he would readily admit, by far the most high-maintenance person in our house. And my mother was the one who indulged him.

She, being a coffee drinker, never had any complaints about her Waffle House meals. But dad, the tea-drinking-prince, who brought his own teabag and ground cardamom to breakfast, often sent our confused waitress back to fetch a cup of *boiling* water, not the kept-tepid-on-a-hot-plate stuff they were bringing him. Like much of my father's culinary fussiness, it was alternately amusing and embarrassing. Finally, he got so tired of improperly steeped teabags accompanying his waffles that he also started bringing his own thermos of water to Waffle House, requiring him to request only a mug of our waitress.

And his demand for a proper cup of tea did not waver, no matter where he was—many a piece of photographic evidence exists to show my father, in the company of the Arkansas group, sitting on a wooden deck at one state park or another, drinking his tea out of a ceramic cup while everyone else sips out of Styrofoam. Of course, most of the credit is due to my mother, who indulgently enabled my father's habits, learning how to rinse and rig coffee machines to bring hotel water to a boil, and at home maintaining the practice of pre-heating both the teapot and my father's mug with the first round of boiling water, before boiling a second pot with which to brew the actual tea. It was she who dutifully put the kettle on when she heard my father stirring from his weekend afternoon naps.

Growing up, I did not realize that my mother's nickname for my father—"*raje*"—meant "prince" or "king." Now that is what she calls my son.

8

Arkansas Group

To have grown up a first-generation Indian kid is to have said "I can't, my parents won't let me," more times than any of the rest of your friends, while at the same time being unable to imagine bad-mouthing your parents like they did theirs. It's to have traded your lunch of spicy tomato rice for something more "normal," like a ham sandwich, to have had your ears pierced as a baby while your classmates begged their parents to pierce theirs at twelve or thirteen. It's to not get paid money for As, like other kids do, or get paid for doing chores around the house, because in your house, no one is rewarded for doing what's expected. It's to be the often unwilling and always unqualified expert on all things related to India, even though you weren't born there and have only visited a few times. It's to be told by your parents, "You have to work twice as hard as everybody else to prove yourself. You don't want people to think you achieved something just because you're brown."

As an adult, it's to walk into a yoga class and cringe when the white girl instructor pronounces the Sanskrit terms badly and adds her own incorrect interpretation to an explanation of the term *namaste*. It's to laugh when food magazines and blogs start writing about how easy it is to make yogurt at home, like this is some kind of revelation, because you've been eating your mom's tangy, plain yogurt since you were a girl. It's to roll your eyes when hipsters sing the praises of ghee and Ayuervedic medicine, and then to catch them wearing bindis and bracelets with mantras on them, the meanings of which they have not bothered to learn. It's to sheepishly look up the foods you've eaten your whole life on the internet because you know how to make them but you don't know what they're called. It's to raise your own children in just as strict a fashion as you were raised, then watch your parents become the world's most indulgent, discipline-averse grandparents, urging you "Don't be so hard on them!" as you recall the amount of misbehavior you were permitted (none) and number of desserts you were allowed to have (one per week).

It's to be among the white people but not of them. It's to be among the brown people but not of them either. It's to try and figure out what it means to think both ways, to worry whether you are too much on one side or the other. It's to meet white people who speak better Hindi than you do, and to feel guilty about that. It's to carry on the traditions you grew up with—prayer altar in the home, occasional trips to the temple, new clothes on Diwali, fasting on the right days, cooking special food on others—but to feel at least a little bit like a fraud when doing it all. It's to marvel at just how different your childhood was from that of the people who raised you, because they worked hard to make it so. It's to think of what your parents have seen, what they've sacrificed, and how hard they've worked, and to know that you'll never have to push quite that hard, because they did. It's to swim in the water you grew up swimming in, and then one day to realize just how good that water is.

I grew up surrounded by an incredibly tight network of "uncles" and "aunties" who, like my parents, emigrated from India in the late sixties and early seventies, following the 1965 removal of the so-called "quota system" from American immigration policy. My fellow first generation children and I, born in the seventies and early eighties, are the reasons that our parents applied for permanent citizenship, and by now they've lived in the United States longer than they ever did India. Though they did not know each other beforehand, are not even from the same region of India, do not necessarily speak each other's native languages or share family background, are from different castes and, in some cases, different religious traditions, our parents raised us together, a makeshift village, in the suburbs of Memphis, Tennessee.

They made it a point, as good immigrant parents do, to put us in the best schools they could find and afford, which in Memphis at that time meant private schools, and Christian ones at that. Given the incredibly diverse religious landscape of India and the fact that many of our parents had been educated by Christians themselves, there was never any objection to the religious context of our schooling, but it did present the logistical problem of what to do when we kids were out of school on holidays that our families didn't celebrate (and *in* school on holidays that we did). An idea emerged one year for Easter break; our parents decided to pile us into cars and drive to an Arkansas state park for the weekend. A tradition was born. We switched state parks each year, but the basic formula remained the same: rooms with bunk beds, campfires outside, hiking, canoe rides, mostly unsuccessful fishing, us kids playing bad 90s music on the boom box, only to have it co-opted by our parents who played old Bollywood songs that we kids pretended not to like.

The uncles taught us to play blackjack with our spare change, telling us that they would donate the house's profits to the local Hindu temple, thereby cancelling out any negative karma incurred by encouraging us to gamble. The aunties brought grocery sacks and ice chests full of food—supplies for morning *chai*, batter and filling for enough *masala dosas* to feed an army, plus plenty of homemade goodies, chutneys, and pickles for all-hours snacking: post-hike, post-nap, late night. At some point, our families became known as the Arkansas Group: Karkera, Kumar, Mehta, Mehra, Rao, Rao, & Vasu. They are my half-dozen extra sets of parents, and the nearly dozen siblings and cousins who aren't technically mine.

Part of what it means to be a family, as far as I can tell, is to be a witness to the particular way someone grew up, someone who shares that particular little pocket of time, place, and circumstance, who knows the inside jokes, shares face time in photographs, who remembers the accidents, the sadness, the difficulty, the tradition, and the joy. So I say that these people, though we are not bound by one drop of blood or any kind of relatedness that would hold up in court, *are* my family.

As a child, my "real" family—all in India—was distant, strange, unfamiliar; I have only visited there three times in my entire life. To me, the people I felt connected to, unconditionally loved by, and stuck with, for better or worse, were the people my parents had chosen, the people whose houses I could ride my bike to, in whose upstairs rooms I played "Taboo" and watched, regrettably, *The Shining* at a very early age. They call me "Nishtie." They *know* me. To this day, when people ask about my family, I speak first about people I'm not related to: the family my parents chose for themselves, and the family I have built for myself as an adult.

I am flying home for my "little sister" Varsha's wedding, my suitcase stuffed full of saris and shoes: four pairs of heels, as instructed by my mother. "Bring a bunch of different colors," she told me via text, "Black, gold, beige, etc. to go with different things." All of my good jewelry, most of which has been bequeathed to me by her, is safely tucked into my carry-on. My hair has been recently trimmed, and I'm good on makeup (application of eyeliner is practically a competitive sport among Indian girls), though I will need to do something about my nails once I arrive.

Varsha, of course, is not actually my little sister—we aren't related at all, at least not by blood. But she and her sister Megha are undeniably my family; our parents have been friends since before any of us were born, and for years we shared weekend slumber parties, alternating houses, building fabulous bed sheet tents, and watching *Home Alone* and *Girls Just Want To Have Fun* over and over and over again. We carpooled to the same school, trick-or-treated together, bickered over stolen candy, formed a "secret" club with dues that none of its members could afford to pay, took classical Indian dance classes and begrudgingly performed the routine in front of our mostly white classmates during "Diversity Week" at school. Our families went on joint vacations—to the Bahamas where we got our hair braided and felt incredibly glamorous, and then on a tour of state parks out west (Yellowstone, Grand Teton, & Glacier National) when we were all in middle school and spent long, often grumpy hours in the rented van trying to ignore our parents who were enthusiastically pointing out the window at scenery! and wildlife! We have witnessed each other's awkward stages, indulged strange obsessions and crushes, driven each other crazy, resented and also cheered each other's accomplishments, nursed each other's ambitions, and "choreographed" many a dance to Billy Joel songs. I know their mom's "I mean business, young lady" tone of voice and their dad's corny jokes as well as I know those of my own parents.

Somehow, we have managed to grow up and become women who genuinely love each other and choose each other, choose to stay friends. Though we all now live in different places, have families and friend groups and interests of our own, there is still a true, extant bond that remains, a kind of love and understanding that can only come when you've shared as much time and space as we have.

Varsha's wedding festivities will consist of four parts—a mendhi (henna) party on Thursday night, a sangeet (music & dancing) party on Friday night, the actual wedding ceremony on Saturday morning, and the wedding reception Saturday night. At each of these events, a full meal will be served, and the number of people invited will range from one to five hundred. Being a member of the extended family means that my mother and I will be attending all four events, and that I will need to have a different sari, hairstyle, and set of jewelry for each one. As soon as I arrive home from my post-flight trip to the gym, my mom and I break down the cache of saris we have compiled—new ones purchased in India by the bride's family and gifted to us, my mom's classic "dowry" pieces, and saris that I have brought from my stash. We divvy up pieces, laying necklaces against the bright fabric, my mother *tsking* when I try to opt down on jewelry: "That's not a heavy enough necklace—it's white people heavy, but in India they'd wear that just sitting around for lunch."

I laugh, aware of how ridiculous all this would seem to my non-Indian friends. But these are just the unspoken rules of how things work. Maniacal as they sound, the truth is, it's fun to live by these rules occasionally—when they're optional. So much of why our parents left India was to get away from norms that felt outdated and oppressive; but while they have adjusted and tempered these norms, they haven't given them up entirely. We, the first-generation children, will carry many of them on ourselves, though our tastes and understanding of what "being Indian" looks like have been undeniably influenced by growing up here. Varsha and her sister Megha (who is also getting married, later this year) both opted to buy costume jewelry instead of the "real thing" for the large pieces they are wearing with the elaborate saris they'll sport at each event. A small detail, perhaps, but indicative of the ways we are figuring out what it means to be hyphenated: first-generation, Indian-American. Now that we are starting our own families, finding partners, raising kids, our traditions are important to us, but they are not the same lifelines they were for our parents. They were young and thousands of miles away from their families, aching for a good Indian meal they didn't have to cook themselves, working and saving and being eyed suspiciously and called "foreigners." For us, the struggle is not the same.

Our parents raised us with a moderate slant, somewhere in between the poles of clinging to the old country and total assimilation. You could always spot the kids whose parents didn't, who came from one of the more "extreme" social circles and showed up at big gatherings of the India Association or at temple celebrations. There were the Westernized kids who never wore Indian clothes, girls in too much makeup and boys with one ear pierced rebelliously, who would all grumble and complain about "having" to eat Indian food, requesting utensils instead of eating with their hands, the Indian way. The super-Indian kids, on the other hand, kept to themselves and were mostly quiet, or at least didn't have much to say to *us*, since we were not "up" on all the latest Bollywood film stars, did not go to the same religious "Sunday school" as them, and actually hung out with white people.

In my little group, we were raised with plenty of connections to our culture— through food, religion, dress, customs, communal celebrations—and we were expected to be proud of and knowledge-able about our heritage. At the same time, I never got the sense that our parents were afraid of us becoming "too American" or were attempting to shelter us from the world at large. On the one hand, they did not compromise on values that, to some of our non-Indian counterparts, seemed strange, but on the other, they encouraged us to explore what interested us, whether it was distinctly "Indian" or not. I marvel at how well they did with this balance, how well-adjusted we all turned out to be. All of us remain committed to maintaining some cultural connection, though we know we can never do it quite like our parents did.

We gained richly by our parents' decision to settle here: oppor-tunity, choice, a broader range of possibilities. But in translation, things are lost: language, rigor, meaning. We are American by birth and Indian by extension.

My girlhood memories are dotted with dinner parties, festive week-end gatherings of the Indian immigrant community I grew up in. The scene plays out like this: in a suburban neighborhood a congre-gation of cars grows rapidly on both sides of a street named after some species of tree, like Willow or Oak or Maple. The sky is dark, and by 8:00 or 8:30 things are getting underway. Women wrapped in brilliantly colored saris of yellow, violet, and turquoise herd their reluctant children up a circle drive while their husbands (dressed in American clothes) balance Corningware dishes full of vegetable *sabji*, stacks of foil-wrapped *roti*, and crock pots full of hot *daal*. The women have cooked all day, each making enough of their specialty to feed about forty people, maybe more. After cooking, they had to dig through their cedar closet, into Indian suitcases decades old. The smell of mothballs, which keep the yards of silk safe, wafted into the open hallway while the women searched for a sari with just the right amount of silverwork, neither too heavy, nor too plain. Then it had to be ironed, all seven yards of it, and the children had to be coaxed into picking something from the hallway closet for themselves. (Invariably, a mother or two lost this battle and her child would arrive, triumphantly, in blue jeans.)

Then there is the issue of timing. Though tonight's guests were told via phone to arrive around seven, they do not dare show before eight, eight-thirty to be safe. Arriving any earlier, they would have found a darkened doorway and a frantic, halfway-dressed hostess. Indian Standard Time always runs at least an hour behind. When families do arrive, they push through the unlocked door without ringing a bell, assured by the pile of shoes and sounds of Hindi music that they are at the right house. Mothers move into the kitchen with their steaming dishes, adding last-minute pinches of cilantro, warming up their curries on the stove. Fathers congregate in the living room with highball glasses of Scotch, wearing pants they've had since graduate school, butter yellow or navy blue, that flare down to the ground over their bare feet. Children, left to their own devices, head upstairs to find a TV. They hold court with a movie which some of them probably aren't allowed to watch until they are summoned downstairs into the dining room. A clock on the stairwell shows nine-thirty; finally, it's time to eat.

Piles of food, mountains of it. Dish after dish of spicy *gobi* (cauliflower), *aaloo* (potatoes) in gravy, soft, steaming rice with cumin, warm rounds of just-made bread, and giant bowls full of home-made *dahi* (yogurt). It's all piled precariously on disposable plates, the heavy-duty kind with Styrofoam partitions, and eaten with hands and lots of napkins. After firsts and seconds, the women make *chai*, Indian tea boiled with milk, cinnamon, cardamom, clove, fennel, star anise, ginger, and black pepper in a giant pot on the stove. Some of the kids are in their mother's lap by now, heads folded onto the slippery cloth, eyes drowsy. Men and women sit on the floor of the living room and sing, old songs with meanings their children do not know. It is close to midnight, at the earliest, when everyone goes home. The little ones pretend to be asleep so that their fathers will carry them to the car.

This was my second life, my "other" world, separate from school and piano lessons and white friends and their church youth groups. This was the world our parents created for us on American soil, traditions they brought over from India, traditions they borrowed from here, some they just plain made up as they went along.

In times of crisis, you learn what your community is for, what it's capable of, and in the weeks of my father's illness and death, the Arkansas Group was nothing short of a wonder. They called doctors, wrote checks, made arrangements, cooked food, visited the hospital, cried with us, comforted us, and loved us, fiercely, in everything that they did. Traditionally, it is marriage that transforms you into an adult in the eyes of the community, but burying your father will do it, too. I know that the way I handled myself in that time bought me a new level of respect among my uncles and aunties; ever since then, they speak to me as an equal, and I am proud of nothing more than I am of that.

The Arkansas Group continued to take the most exquisite, indefatigable care of my mother in the months and years following my father's death; the main reason I felt like I didn't have to drop my life and to move back to Memphis was knowing that she was in their hands. Mind you, my mother is not an easy person to care for—she is stubborn, fiercely independent, and *hates* asking for help. She is not social the way my father was, rather the opposite, lone wolf and introvert. I think she was actually a little bit surprised by how genuine and steadfast these friends' attentions to her were, since my father was the one that had been the life of the party, the extroverted volunteer. But true friends are true friends, and our friends called to check on her, brought her food, invited her out to dinner and the movies, even when she almost always refused. They stuck with her.

Which made me terrified to come out to them. Though I was out to almost everyone else in my life, and had told most of my fellow first-generation children, all of whom had been supportive, I didn't know how the older generation would react. My gratitude toward them and the level of closeness I had reached with them in the wake of my father's death made it even scarier: so much more to lose. My own parents had struggled mightily with my sexuality; my father died before he managed to come terms with it, and since then my mother had been trying, but still struggling. Jill, my partner, had visited Memphis a few times, introduced as my "friend," but I felt that some of the Arkansas Group probably *knew*. I wanted to respect my mother, who was grieving deeply and reticent to speak about my sexuality, but I didn't want to hide anymore, not from these people I respected so much.

One night at dinner, about a year-and-a-half after my father's death the Arkansas Group told my mom that they didn't care that I was gay—that they understood her disappointment, but that they still loved me, knew I was a good person—so when did they get to meet Jill? And did she like Indian food?

When we were girls, we were all pretty sure that our parents would freak out if we ever brought home a boy who wasn't brown, would never have dreamed of sharing a room in our parents' house with aforementioned boy if we weren't married to him, and certainly none of us *ever* contemplated what might happen should one us of turn out to be gay. But America changed our parents in ways they hadn't expected it to; so much has happened that our parents hadn't planned and they have weathered it. Their daughters lived with boyfriends before getting married, their sons married white girls, and a handful of us even pursued paths other than the stereotypically acceptable-for-Asian "doctor" or "engineer."

At the first of Varsha's wedding events, I weave through the crowd of bright colors, hugging in greeting the uncles and aunties I have not seen in a while, inquiring about kids and grandkids, sons and daughters-in-law. I am greeted warmly—welcomed, included, loved—and fussed at only because I am there alone. "Where's Jill?" everyone asks, to which I respond, "What, *I'm* not enough?" pretending to be annoyed but more grateful than I can say for their teasing. I was so prepared to be the black sheep that it's disarming to feel such a part of things, at home again in my family of choice, no longer compartmentalizing major pieces of my life.

As far as Jill goes, they seem to have applied to her the same criteria they always had for the people they wanted us to grow up and marry: she is smart, successful, ambitious, close to her own family, respectful of mine, and she loves me very much. It helps that she does, in fact, like Indian food, and has a "brown people" spice tolerance. (The aunties love that part, especially.) When Jill fought cancer last year, we received regular cards and emails from the Arkansas group—they were praying for her, they loved us. And when mail from them arrives at my house now, wedding invitations, birth announcements, holiday cards, it arrives addressed to us both.

Part of what it means to be brown is that we do things differently. We think a two-hundred person wedding is "small," that having a "few people" over for dinner means 15-20, and we say "I just made some food, nothing fancy," when what we've done is whip up three dishes, rice, homemade bread, yogurt, and a dessert. Our moms are Tiger moms, so no, we can't actually come out with you on Friday night, and our dads learned to love American football as a substitute for their beloved cricket, to which they had no televised access when they first moved here. As kids, being brown meant that friends always wanted to come over to our house, because our moms cooked food that other moms didn't, and were always happy to hand out plates to the white girls, telling them to "Eat, eat, so skinny!" then send them out the door with leftovers packed into recycled Cool Whip containers and bundled into a plastic sack.

When I graduated from high school, my parents threw me a party. All of my white girl classmates were there, in J. Crew and Banana Republic dresses, mingling with the "other side" of my life, my extended Indian family. An Indian food restaurant was catering the party, and for the first hour, an array of appetizers was set out: *samosas, bhel puri, pakoras.* My classmates kept going back for seconds and thirds, sheepish at first, then eating unabashedly. After a little while, my mother realized what was going on. "They thought that was going to be the whole meal! That this was all we were going to serve! Like those American parties where they give you four little canapés and some grapes and expect you to survive on that!"

I had to announce to my friends that there was more food on the way—and how—big hotel trays full of steaming rice, chicken curry, *saag paneer, channa, naan.* There are pictures in my graduation album of my friends all lined up, piling their plates full, faces betraying astonishment over the sheer quantity of food. My friend Jenny, who is the Platonic ideal of genuine, well-bred Southern belle, even sent my parents a thank-you note afterward: "[the party] was such a refreshing change from the usual cheese and fruit."

If it comes down to a choice between under-expressing and over-expressing, not having enough to eat or having too much, a quiet party or a loud one, a house looking like museum or looking like people actually live there, people pretending like nothing's wrong or people being all up in your business, well, you can guess which side I'm on.

I love wearing saris. Being a bigger-than-the-average-Indian girl— I'm 5' 7" and a size 10—I grew up feeling like a giant next to most of the petite Indian girls I grew up with, so it's exciting for me that in a sari, my curves are actually an advantage. For the day of Varsha's actual wedding, I get to wear two new saris: a simple, elegant red one with a circular gold pattern for the religious ceremony that takes place in the morning, and a bright teal, heavily beaded-and-mirrored sari for the evening reception, at which I will be emceeing along with the groom's brother. Add to that two different hair styles, plenty of make-up, and a gaudy-by-Western-standards, practically-modest-by-Indian-standards-amount of gold jewelry, including earrings borrowed from my mom with posts so wide that I have to literally screw them into my ears and ignore a little blood.

The morning's ceremony includes the *baraat* (in which the groom arrived on horseback, surrounded by his family, who dance and play drums in celebration), a *puja* (invocation of the gods) to bless the marriage, procession of the bride (who is, according to tradition, supposed to keep her eyes down, demure and modest), and a complex, multi-part religious ceremony performed in Sanskrit by a priest, in which both the brides' and the grooms' parents participate, fusing not only the couple but the two families for life. After the marriage is made official, a giant lunch buffet is served. Start-to-finish duration? Approximately four hours.

That evening, we all return to the Hilton, the only Memphis venue big enough to hold the expected crowd and also willing to accommodate outside catering: asking a non-Indian crew to cook Indian food is a recipe for disaster. Cocktail hour has begun, complete with a generous buffet of "snacks" that easily rivals the spread I've seen at most white people weddings: everything from chilled shrimp to tandoori lamb to huge displays of cheese and fruit. There will be a full dinner served later, of course, and a dessert buffet, as well. My Shaila Aunty, Varsha and Megha's mother, is a woman of impeccable taste, crazy-organized and formidable; she is a fixture of the Memphis philanthropic community and knows everyone in the Memphis Indian community—this is a wedding to end all weddings, make no mistake about it.

Everyone is dressed in their finest and fanciest, even my mother, who has avoided wearing saris since my father died. I am nervous but excited to be a part of the reception; I was honored when Varsha asked, and want to do her, and my second family, a credit. Since the groom's family is from Gujarat, a state in Western India, my mom helped me wear my sari, which was a gift from Shaila Aunty, *seedha pallu* style, the typical Gujarati way in which the *pallu*, or most ornate section of the sari is pulled up over the *seedha*, or right, shoulder and fanned out over the torso. We are not Gujarati, so we didn't really know what we were doing, but I thought we had managed to get the job done. Apparently not, for as the crowd files in, the Gujarati aunties descend.

"Nishtie, Nishtie, you look so beautiful but this sari is all messed up." Their tongues cluck as they start to lift up my pleats and fabric, assessing. I am standing between my mother and a buffet table, gin and tonic in hand, in full view of the public, but they don't seem to mind.

"*Tsk, tsk,* too many pins," one of the aunties decides, setting her drink down on a nearby table. "Here," she says, turning me around, and the rearranging begins.

This continues for about five minutes, three women tucking, folding, smoothing, and re-pinning, my mom standing by, looking bemused. The Aunties do not move me into the bathroom; they do not even move me away from the ever-growing line of people waiting nearby for the open bar. They just continue their work until they are satisfied, then hand me the excess pins, pick up their drinks, tell my mother what a sweet, pretty girl I am, and walk away. I could pick these women out of a lineup, but I couldn't tell you their names to save my life. That's just how we brown people roll.

Here's what you need to know about the village that raised me: they are all completely insane. I'm serious. They are warm and generous, hilariously funny, smart, and some of the straight-up best human beings I know. But they're also nuts. Crazy-late-night-Indian-music-party people, crazy-Uncles-dressed-in-drag-and-lip-synching, crazy-loud-opinionated-aunties, crazy, crazy, crazy.

I happened to be in town a few summers ago for my Priya Aunty's sixtieth birthday. Since I was the only "kid" present, I had the pleasure of witnessing our parents at their finest, and sneakiest. They wanted to surprise Priya Aunty by pretending to blow off her birthday, and then showing up in her backyard with fireworks and dinner. So we gathered at dusk just down the street from Aunty's house at another Arkansas Group family's home, where Ashok Uncle, always the master of such schemes, had brigadiered a whole set of plans.

"Nishtie, you're in charge of the smoke bombs, okay?"

"Um, okay." He thrust several packages of the brightly colored devices, which looked just exactly like miniature versions of stereotypical TV cartoon bombs, except they weren't black.

"Light as many as you can and throw them into the backyard—the women are in charge of the smoke, the men will set off the Black Cats."

Eyeing the grocery bags lined up behind him, I ventured, "Wait, how much of this stuff did you buy? How much *is* there?"

Uncle feigned a guileless face as his wife, Bina Aunty chimed in, "Oh Nisht, this is only half of what there was. You should have seen what we had for the Fourth!"

As we waited for the last family to arrive, all of the food was loaded up into Bina Aunty's car to make for easy transport. Cooking was done in potluck fashion; each dish had been pre-assigned based on the Aunty's specialty. They've stopped bending-over-backwards to cook up outrageous, coordinated feasts like they did in my youth.

At last we marched over, fireworks and matches in hand, and sneaked into the backyard. This was the perfect set-up because the house has a lovely back addition with nearly floor-to-ceiling windows looking out onto the yard. Giggling, we set off and threw smoke bombs towards the center of the lawn, causing plumes of brilliantly colored smoke, aqua, green, purple, yellow, and blue, to form in the air.

"It looks like Holi," someone said, and indeed, I was reminded of our favorite childhood holiday, which commemorates spring and fertility and joy. On that day, people gather in large groups to throw powdered pigment on each other, reflecting the colors of the season. Kids fill their water-guns with thinned paint, everyone runs, shouts, laughs, dances.

Of course, when a few of the Uncles began lighting Black Cats on the pathway, the ear-splitting, machine-gun-mimicking noise took a tiny bit away from the claim that we were recreating a sacred holiday, but the overall effect was still pretty incredible. I laughed so hard that I could barely keep up with my smoke-bomb lighting duties, holding out match after match for the Aunties. Soon we saw Priya Aunty at the back door. I waved. Her face was priceless.

Priya Aunty's husband, Bhaskar Uncle is a brilliant pediatric surgical oncologist and the quietest of the uncles, perhaps because his wife is the loudest of the aunties. Our "inside man" on the surprise scheme, Uncle had told Aunty that he made reservations at a nearby Italian restaurant for the two of them for dinner and sent her upstairs to put on make-up. She had just come back downstairs when she spotted intruders creeping across her driveway. She immediately locked the back door and called for Bhaskar Uncle—I think we're pretty lucky she didn't call the police.

Priya Aunty has this great South Indian accent which means her inflection is always going up and her words are strung together just an edge too fast. She makes killer *dosas*, of which I have eaten hundreds in my time, and used to pinch my cheeks the hardest when I was a little girl.

Before we could eat dinner (I had bet Mom it would be nine o'clock before we ate, and I was right), Ashok Uncle sat us all down in the living room for a presentation. The man certainly has a flair for the dramatic. He's a psychiatrist by profession, and I've long possessed a preoccupied curiosity regarding what he must be like with his patients. Because he's so loony with us, I suspect he must save the professional Dr. Jekyll for his clinical practice.

Ashok Uncle has always been the fun one. He's the one we wanted to ride with on our Arkansas trips, because he would playfully swerve the car on deserted roads or stop and buy us candy at the gas station. He'd yell "Look, a peacock!" while pointing out the Jeep window and we'd all fall for it. He's convinced all of us, adults and children alike, to believe or do something ridiculous at least once. My mother used to be one of his favorite targets; on one trip, he turned down her cabin's sheets before bed and left mints on the pillow. "Can you believe it? I didn't think they'd do that all the way out here!" Mom showed everyone her mints before someone's laughter gave it away. On another trip, the adults were hiking when Ashok ran back to the group with the news that he'd spotted a tamarind tree in the Arkansas forest. To prove it, he'd brought a raw tamarind pod with him (purchased at the Vietnamese grocery in Memphis a few days before). My mom, who loves sour fruit and used to suck on tamarinds as a child, literally jumped up and down with excitement before the joke was revealed. She loves telling that story.

Since my dad's death, Ashok Uncle doesn't tease mom as much anymore, or argue with her about politics, but he does still try to make her laugh. His "presentation" for Priya Aunty consisted of the bestowal of half-a-dozen gag gifts, from breast suspenders to an advice book, *Sex After 60*, in which the pages were all blank. Uncle had warned me beforehand that the gifts were of the PG-13 variety. He knew I would be fine with it, he just didn't want it to make my mom and I uncomfortable to be watching all of this together. He doesn't tease me much anymore, either.

After the variety show, Ashok sought out my mother. "It's good to see you laugh," I heard him say. "I know this is hard for you." If my father were still alive, he would have helped Ashok plan this whole thing. They were generally partners in crime, partners in Scotch. To know my father is missed by everyone, not just us, is a great comfort.

The wedding reception goes swimmingly—first dances, slideshows of embarrassing photographs, toasts, cake-cutting, a musical performance by two of the bride's talented violinist friends, and even a surprise from the bride and groom, an adorable dance to Taylor Swift's "Our Song," replete with cowboy hats and impressive choreography, worthy of going viral of YouTube. My co-emcee and I have successfully completed our duties, and now I am weaving through the ballroom with my highball, stopped at each fabric-swathed and flower-laden table by friends, uncles, and aunties who tell me how "natural" I was. I am pleased, less so out of ego than the fact that this means I will not have let the family down.

Too hyped to be hungry, I visit with out-of-town guests, the "big brothers" and "big sisters" I grew up with, peering into their iPhones for the latest pictures of kiddos, updating them on Jill's health and our plans to adopt. The bride and groom find me, hug and thank me as I sneak them a plate of their own desserts (which they are too crowded with people to go get themselves). "I'm ready to get this party started," I tell them. "When do we dance?"

It is something of an unspoken rule at Indian weddings; the couple isn't *really* married until you get up and dance. We are an expressive, perhaps over-expressive people, and we do not have a "tame" or "halfway" version of things; our rituals are colorful and loud and multi-sensory, and when we have a wedding, we *have a wedding.*

Within minutes, the lights have been dimmed and the dance floor cleared, and the DJ is tossing out Indian dance songs that I and my Punjabi shoulder-popping dancing genes just can't resist. Joining the small crowd on the dance floor, I start twirling in earnest, catching the faces of Arkansas Group uncles and aunties around me, joyful because Varsha got married today and I was there. Men and women dance around me—mostly brown people at this point, with a few brave Westerners taking on the Indian rhythm.

Suddenly I see my mom's hot pink sari coming toward me, her left arm posed gracefully above her head and her right hand on her hip. I freeze and do a double-take; I haven't seen my mother dance in years, since before my father died. I watch her, staring.

I had forgotten what a good dancer she is, too, elegant and light on her feet, not at all self-conscious and still sexy at almost sixty-five. The uncles and aunties around me look surprised as well; it's no secret how reserved and closed-down she has been in the last few years, but here she is, shaking her hips in front of everyone, plain as day, and in this moment, I could not love her more. I move closer and we dance together, singing the lyrics of "*Sona, Sona*," the infectious Punjabi-style wedding song from the late nineties that's playing, to each other. My mom looks happier than I have seen in a long, long time, and all I can think of is how proud I am of her, how proud my father would be, what guts and moxie she's showing, like the old days. She catches the shocked look on my face and leans over to explain into my ear: "I had to dance. My daughter got married today."

9

What Light

At the service, I am surprised to see that the "hymn" we will be singing in unison is ubiquitous, hold-up-your-lighters "Let It Be." I am surprised because I know that Dave was against the thought of having a Beatles song at his sister's funeral—"damn Unitarians," he had grumbled at the possibility, alluding to the church in which he and his sister had grown up. Clearly he was overruled, or at least kept quiet while musical decisions were made.

Dave's parents were not—are not—particularly religious, but the Unitarian church was the structure they chose to introduce their children to the world, and it gave Dave, their youngest, his love for poetry and sense of wonder about nature. Somewhere down the line, though, he became a terrible Anglophile and a bit of a snob, so his taste for ritual grew much more formal than that of the church he was raised in. I spent twelve years at an Episcopalian school myself, so I sympathize with his desire for pomp and circumstance; as it is, Dave and I are almost always in agreement on matters of aesthetics.

I am standing in the back of the room with Phil, a mutual friend of Dave's and mine who met me here in Atlanta for the funeral. We refused seats from the ushers because I want to be in Dave's line of sight when he stands up and faces the crowd. This is the first funeral I've been to since my own father's three-and-a-half years ago. I scan the front row to find the back of Dave's head, his particular swirl of blond hair instantly recognizable to me. I focus my whole being on that head.

The surrounding walls are salmon pink and bad artwork hangs in an alarmingly haphazard fashion along the staircase that leads down to the room where we all have gathered. We are cocooned into the base of a hill, the room's back wall one big window, which we the funeral audience face. Oak trees and good Southern grass stand in the red glow of Atlanta sunset, and it strikes me as a particular kindness to have a window to look out of right now, the landscape scrambling with squirrels and robins and a million unseen living things.

Despite my disdain for "Let It Be" and the fact that I've heard it so many times before, when the piano plays the opening chords, my tears come. Phil pulls me into his shoulder, which is bony and hard and which I reach only because I am wearing heels. He holds the program up so that we can sing dozens of "Let it bes," following the printed lyrics, the refrain transforming into a kind of chant, blurring at the edges between understanding and jibberish, the way a word starts to lose its meaning when you type it over and over.

In my religion, Hinduism, as in many others, we sing. We sing loud, robust, and rhythmic, in a language no one really speaks anymore and that few people actually understand. We sing, and we repeat. This ritual of repetition is magical, deceptive in its simplicity. It is easy to disregard the power that words can have to lull us into a liminal space, to loop and circle around us until they are almost tangible.

Words in the form of mantras are supposed to have the power to unlock truth, not because they themselves are necessarily true, but because of the space they force the chanter into, the state of mind or openness of soul. And though I was so uninspired by its inclusion just minutes before, I find now that this overused Beatles song is having the same effect on me: Let it be. Let it be. Let it be. Let it be. I will never be able to hear this song the same way again.

When the singing stops, my best friend gets up to eulogize his sister and my whole body pulses with the desire to ease his pain.

David Allen Berry is one of the few people I will walk through a museum with. I trust him also at the theatre, the opera, or as a companion for serious film. He knows that I crave space; I do not want to talk about what I've seen when I've only just seen it. I like, instead, to walk to the car, talking of other things, people watching, laughing, and then to drive somewhere for dinner and find a quiet table and a glass of wine or Scotch, and rock it gently from side to side while discussing politics, work, books, what we've done since we saw each other last. We will order a pizza to share, and a bowl of glistening olives to occupy our stomachs in the meantime. And just about the time our second glasses of wine are poured, then I am ready to pick apart the art.

The cultivation of this rhythm began the first evening I ever spent with Dave, as a teenager in a cornfield in east Tennessee. There aren't many cornfields in Tennessee, and this was a very small one, an agricultural experiment on the campus of The University of Tennessee, Martin. Martin is about as small and middle-of-nowhere as it gets, the kind of place where it's easy to imagine college students tapping kegs and tipping cows and devolving into small circles of pleasure and interest. A strange place to send soon-to-be-high-school seniors for a summer program, but there we were.

Dave and I did not spend much time together during those six weeks, at least not directly; we traveled in close but separate circles, a Venn diagram of relationship overlap. But on that last night we began our friendship, even though, at the time, we didn't know that was what we were doing. Nobody slept that night; curfew was lifted and we were allowed to order bad Chinese takeout, drop Cokes from the vending machines, sign each other's "yearbooks" and talk and talk, the very act creating its own significance in our minds, the conversation more profound in memory than I'm sure it actually was.

I developed a significant crush on Dave that night, as we sat in a cornfield with others, talking until the sun came up. He fit the profile of my attraction perfectly—incredibly smart white boy who cared about ideas and books but was slightly socially oblivious, which kept him from being too intimidating. I did not act on my crush; I happened to know he was interested in someone else in the program, and we were leaving the next day anyway: Dave to Oak Ridge and I to Memphis. A few weeks later, somewhat boldly, I sent him a mix tape and a letter, because that was what you did when you liked somebody. He wrote back, a brief letter in what I now know to be an exceptionally readable sample of his handwriting, with a poem he had composed in accompaniment. It was a kind gesture, but made his lack of romantic interest clear. I did not write him back.

The following summer, I received an email from Dave saying that he had heard through mutual friends that I would be starting at Rice University in the fall. He would be as well, following in his sister Diane's footsteps, as she had just graduated that spring. Our families ran into each other on move-in day; Dave and I had been placed in the same dorm and he was the only person I even remotely knew in all of Texas.

We soon assumed an intimacy that picked up several paces ahead of where we had left off, because the neutral zone of unfamiliar territory made even our tangential connection seem significant. I no longer pined after him—I had taken to dating girls in the interim—so instead I was free to learn him and let him learn me, at the same time we were both trying to figure ourselves out. Dave quickly became grafted into my little group of friends, which quickly became *our* group of friends. He is present in nearly every college memory I have: sitting on the floor of my dorm room, listening to CDs, mixing dreadfully cheap vodka into lemon drops before the Sadie Hawkins dance, eating pancakes at IHOP at two in the morning.

When he studied abroad fall semester of our junior year, I missed him more than I had planned on. We emailed often, and the distance cemented our closeness, building on how much we knew of each other, how much we liked each other, all the way down to the core. In the spring, he returned, and we spent nearly all of that semester together. Our friends took to calling him my "fake boyfriend."

In January of 2010, I received a text message from Dave: "Diane was in Haiti. For work. She's missing. Flying to TN tonight." Texting is today's telegraph, it would seem, suited to the context of crisis, terse and unromantic, dampening the potential for melodrama, curbing the recipient's temptation to flurry into a coo of words.

The photograph Dave's family sent to the media, which I found, in a daze, on the website of the *New York Times*, was taken in my house. Diane worked for the Centers for Disease Control and was in Haiti to observe and help with the AIDS relief work they do there. It was a trip she volunteered to go on. She and her husband Jeff had visited Houston just a few months before, to see Dave and his new house. It happened to be the same weekend as the party my partner Jill and I throw each year to commemorate *Diwali*, the Hindu Festival of Lights. Having met Diane and Jeff some five years before, at mine and Dave's college graduation, I encouraged him to bring them along to the party.

Ours is a big *fête*, house full of folks and food; Diwali is an unabashedly celebratory holiday, no fasting, no hours at temple required. The holiday is centered around a homecoming, that of the god Rama, who was in exile for many years, searching for his abducted wife and fighting against the forces of evil. According to our mythology, the night he returned, the villagers of Ayodhya lit his pathway with little oil lamps, now symbols of a holiday that celebrates the triumph of good over evil, the victory of light over dark.

On Diwali, it's traditional to wear bright colors, and preferably new clothes, to match the spirit of the holiday. So, in what turned out to be one of the last photographs ever taken of Diane, she is sporting an orange cap sleeved shirt, holding a red plastic party cup and smiling in my living room. Dave is in the background in a pink polo, and right behind him, Jeff in green. Their eyes are not looking at the camera, but rather at me, outside the shot, standing off to the side, wrapped up in a sari and making a toast to friends, family, and my father, after whose death I began throwing these parties.

A year after Dave and I graduated from college, my father went to his primary care doctor complaining of what seemed to be a shortness of breath. He died less than three weeks later. The rare, cause-unknown disease he contracted causes the soft tissue of the lungs to harden and has no treatment options. Hospital doctors took so long to correctly diagnose his condition that by the time I heard them say, "We need to start thinking about what your father would want," I felt I knew everything I would ever need to know about what was important and what was not. Clarity, at such a high cost.

"It is a perverse club," Dave wrote to me during his family's long CNN-and-coffee-fueled-vigil, "that no one wants to join but into which we are all inevitably inducted."

Even the *possibility* of death and trauma, long before the actuality of it, baptizes you in a flash, the water teeth-achingly cold. And I watched as Dave broke the surface, every note of my memory resonating as he patterned his sorrow before me. It was impossible not to compare; though a line-by-line did no good, I was still useful in small ways. I knew what to say, or what not to say. I knew to send magazines for daytime attention, books of poetry for the hardest hours of night. I baked and mailed brownies. I felt strangely pleased that my own history with death was at last yielding some concrete utility. Still, in spite of all I knew, there was nothing to be done.

As rescue workers dug, everyone mentally calculated scenarios and hours of daylight and likelihoods. Dave marked time in his parents' house, on leave from his high-paying, spreadsheets-and-meetings job, managing very different sets of information, taking very different kinds of phone calls. After an excruciating limbo and more than one false alarm, it was confirmed; Diane had died in Haiti, in the earthquake, almost exactly one week after her sixth wedding anniversary. She was thirty-one years old.

Loss tugs, as if at the fraying hem of a cutoff pair of jeans, it squeezes and compacts and leaves you breathless, gripping the steering wheel, staring into a canvas, excusing yourself at dinner, unwilling to rise in the morning or unable to sleep at night. Still, in the basest sense, loss is something one possesses. It can be claimed with words—"mine"—and is not questioned. It returns like a boomerang, or a weed you can't manage to get rid of. One's own pain can be worn gracefully; at least, one can learn how to wear it.

One has a right to one's own pain. But regarding the pain of others—which is felt, deeply, but cannot be claimed—we are dashed, and at a loss.

I had an urge to row to Haiti, to tend to the injured but more to steep myself in loss, to inundate myself with the pornography of other people's tragedy. It was a small urge, one of many in a moment or in a lifetime I would disown at Peter's gates. Things are lost, people even, and I am bereft of answers. You write that grief is twitchy and strange. Tell me about that, and tell me a story. Not everything must be lost forever. Love, Phil

When his flight was cancelled because of snow, Phil took a train from New York to Atlanta to attend Diane's funeral. He was dressed not in scrubs, but for clinical work, luckily funeral-appropriate, and he had his wallet, a cell phone, and not much else. In the fifteen minutes before he boarded an Amtrack at Grand Central Station, he worried not about food, but two items that betray so much about him: a novel and a toothbrush. The train trip took eighteen hours.

He met me in the Atlanta airport at the top of the escalators leading up to baggage claim, in one of those perfectly orchestrated moments that's sheer coincidence but feels cinematic. We had not seen each other in three years, during which time he had begun medical school, taken to wearing flat-front pants and hipster glasses, and asked his girlfriend to marry him (she said yes). He wrapped me up in a bear hug and insisted on handling my suitcase.

When I first met Phil at a cramped dorm room party, I couldn't stand him. The second I heard him refer to something as "gay," I pegged him as boorish, crude, and juvenile, and let him have it. I did a lot of that in those days: swift judgments, thorough excoriations. I left the aforementioned party in a huff, convinced that Phil was an idiot.

How seductively easy it is to draw harsh lines with our convictions, strutting righteously through the day's doorways. But I must have trusted Dave enough to know that Phil could not be as awful as I had decided he was. Over time, a tolerance grew. By senior year, I liked him well enough to agree to live with him: Dave, Phil, me, and my closest girl friend Rebecca. 1601 Colquitt was a big, sprawling rental house that had once been split in half, then rejoined together crudely, forcing you to step down at the seam. The sides mirrored each other conveniently, allowing for separate gender bathrooms and providing us with two refrigerators, which meant the boys could devote one entirely to beer.

Aside from my father, I had never shared space with men before. I am an only child, I attended an all-girls' school for twelve years, and the only boyfriend I ever had was just for a few months. So living with Phil and Dave felt like an anthropological study—they wrote brilliant papers but could not load a dishwasher to save their lives. They ate obscene amounts of food, put whey powder in their smoothies, and considerately left their stinky running shoes on the porch. Their bodies were tall and flat and sweaty.

We had family dinner each Sunday, for which Rebecca and I cooked and the boys grocery shopped. I would send them to the store with a list in the morning, keeping my phone on hand for the inevitable "aisle-dilemma" consultations. Most of my memories involve staying up late at night sitting on the blond wood floor of the living room, and talk-talk-talking. Dave reading Machado poems aloud in Spanish, Phil and I watching the Disney version of Robin Hood together.

The letters began after graduation, but came in a steady stream after my father died. Phil sent the first just a few days after the funeral, full of clumsy disclaimers and packaged with his sister's homemade cookies. The stereotypically WASP-y, cream-colored pages of stationery backgrounded beautiful thoughts, thoughts even beyond what late-night talks had previously revealed. Death makes a conversation intimate without anybody having to try.

I felt blurry around the edges then, as if I had been smudged with an eraser, as if I were vibrating, constantly, at the lowest possibly frequency, and that the possibility of my disappearance was real. To press myself into a page in the direction of a half-friend, half-stranger was to throw a tether back down into the world. And so, I wrote him back.

We began to say things—things I could never say anywhere else, certainly not out loud, certainly not face-to-face. Phil's skyscraper-tall handwriting became my familiar; I would impatiently watch the mail for his New York-postmarked envelopes, then tuck them onto my bedside table and force myself to wait, to save them for the end of the day, where I would savor them, banked up on pillows next to Jill, both of us in glasses, she with her *TIME* magazine. Phil and I wrote consistently, changing addresses, starting and finishing grad school, never managing to be in the same place at the same time, but ever on the page together. Our letters, and our friendship, they bloomed.

I am sitting in a circular booth in a moderately bad hotel bar, fake red leather giving off a sports-bar kind of vibe. The bar is dominated by convention-attendees of some kind, or so I assume from the look of the laminated plastic nametags they still wear as they nurse their drinks.

Phil and I arrived about ten o'clock, one beer behind Dave and his father, who is determined to keep up with us kids tonight, the day of his daughter's funeral. We go easy on him, taking it slow. I have ostensibly given up alcohol for Lent, but I drink three beers anyway. "I do not think the Lord will mind, " I tell the table. "There are exceptions, and then there are *exceptions*."

It's been a month since I've had a drink, and this buzz feels particularly nice. Without it, this all feels too real, too strong: so the saying goes about "taking the edge off." Local beer is on tap, otherwise Dave and I would be simultaneously stripping longnecks naked of their labels and shredding them on the lacquered wood table.

I am sitting across the booth from him, so I cannot reach my hand out to rest on his leg for just a moment, or press my shoulder into his, tie him here so he won't float away. I think of what I did the night of my father's funeral—sat on the couch and ate an entire box of Lucky Charms cereal slowly, in handfuls, trying my level best to keep a single thought from running through my head. I was too scared to let myself drink that night, though of what I was afraid I am not sure.

On purpose, I am not wearing the dress I wore that day—I went out to buy a new one, because it seemed to matter. I don't want to have a "funeral dress." I wore my new dress along with hose and heels to the bar, since Phil only has one outfit and I wanted to stay formal in solidarity with him. Like a good Southern girl, I swapped my nude daytime hose for black evening, these things we are somehow trained to do without remembering how we learned them.

"There are so many things being a boy means you don't have to know," Phil marveled, when I explained the reason for the change to him. "Also, that is a very nice dress."

I have learned to translate boy language by now, and so I understood that the compliment should make me grin, and it did. Hose make me love my legs, long and proud. My body starts to shimmer, from the beer and the company, these men I feel possessive of. I become liquid, or rather conscious of just how liquid I am, blood rushing, fluids moving, all beneath the surface. The way I can still manage to be vain at a time like this.

When I get up to go the bathroom, Dave trails behind me. We stand together in the hallway next to the courtesy phone and I look at him, hold his face in my hands. "Hey," he says. "I'm really glad you came."

When I return to the table, all three men are engrossed in passionate conversation about health care, science, and the limits of what can be known. No idle talk in this crowd. We throw out the names of books we've recently read, or read about, or have been meaning to read. And we toast to Diane, clinking Atlanta Falcon glasses underneath a garishly new-and-trendy light fixture. It is Calder-influenced in its makings and my mind darts back to the day's eulogies, in which Diane's father told the story of taking her to the National Gallery as a baby. "I remember her big blue eyes staring up at the giant Calder mobile hanging from the ceiling, so alert and interested. She was only a few months old."

In the bar, I catch his eye and I see that he, too, is thinking of Calder and his little baby girl. He is father minus daughter and I am the inverse of his equation, the way it is supposed to go.

I was in the room when my father died. I gave an order to the nurse to have his respirator removed and I watched as his breaths shortened, then stopped. I pushed the button in the crematorium that sent the box with his body inside on a conveyor belt, deep into a furnace. I was the last person to look at my father before he was turned to ash.

Death profoundly disrupts understandings of space and time. Verb tenses become slippery, frustrating—my father *was* a good man, my father *is* a big influence on my life—both are true, if not technically correct. There are times when I feel my father so profoundly, though I know it's a trick of my own mental conjure. I make myself practice, recalling his voice, his face in a smile, the sound of his singing. I am terrified of experiencing a second loss, one in which I forget things about him, no longer know him anymore.

Each year that passes stacks up a new set of birthdays, accomplishments, and anniversaries for which he is missing. I know it is natural and necessary to grow accustomed to his absence but I prefer to stubbornly resist. I do not know where to find my father now. I do not know where to go looking.

The day after the funeral, Dave's parents treat Phil and I and a hand-ful of visiting family members to brunch. Jeff, a widower now, sits at the end of the table and lets me hug him and urge him "Take care of yourself," even though I have no right to do so. During the meal, I'm wedged into a corner, far away from the guys but next to Dave's mom, so we talk about Emily Dickinson and our favorite breakfast foods and how much I love her son.

After the meal, Phil and I steal Dave away for a walk through the hip, thirty-somethings-with-young kids neighborhood, sidewalks charmingly cracked on the hills, houses Lego-layered, parks well-kept. The morning is sunny and cold, so I tuck my hands into my coat pockets and walk between the men.

If it seems inappropriate that I want to skip down the sidewalk the day after Diane's funeral, consider this: the mechanism of a human being is such that we can hold, for better or worse, myriad states of mind at once. Pleasures of the body distract the grieving mind: a cup of good coffee, the blue, blue sky, desire to touch and be touched. Nerve endings do not cease their work simply because we are sad. Is it perverse that I feel happiness right now? Loss of human life is the reason I am sharing time with two of my favorite people on this earth, so if I could trade Dave's sister back for every raw moment of the weekend—

But bargains don't work like that. I have learned that it is impossi-ble to untangle what is from what could have been, that every moment precipitates necessarily from what has been lost. To attempt to separate is to go mad. And, truth be told, you *want* your life to change com-pletely, to ensure that you'll never be able to cross the "B.C./A.D." line of demarcation that has suddenly appeared, stamped across everything, allowing you to say with confidence, "I will never be the same."

Even witnessing, at close proximity and in regular intervals, the suffering of others does not imbue one with the understanding of what it feels like to deal with disaster oneself. After Diane died, Phil wrote: *I fear I chose medicine because I realized, perhaps only dimly, that to minister to the body is simple compared to the ministry of the mind and soul.*

There is no shame in what he practices; we want to fix what can be fixed, to see with our own eyes the formation of a scar, the removal of a cancer, the setting of bone. But Dave's landscape is unknowable to Phil, and he knows it.

Still, there can be comfort. The three of us know each other without speaking, our silences full and unhurried. When we do talk, it's easy gossip about mutual friends: who will get married next, who likes their job, who will have babies first. We move into more urgent, but still gentle questions—tomorrow's ceremony at the CDC, Dave's flight back to Houston, when he will see his parents next. Rhythm and presence count for more than I might have once bargained.

I spot an especially large gap in the sidewalk up ahead and plant each hand on a different shoulder—my left on Dave's, my right on Phil's—and push myself up over the crevice in a bounce. This day, too, will be lost.

A few weeks after the funeral, Dave and I take a walk through the galleries inside Houston's Menil Collection, paces matched after years of practice. He has never been the affectionate one—it isn't his instinct to hold a hand up to the small of my back or to kiss my cheek when we say goodbye, but he responds when I hug his shoulder, tuck my arm insistently into his. I learned to be insistent with him; it took me years to figure out that he didn't, in fact, mind.

The centerpiece of the exhibit we are here to see is Maurizio Cattelan's sculpture installation *All*. The nine pieces, made entirely of marble, are laid out in a line, vertically intersecting the gallery room which is otherwise empty. Each piece has been molded to depict the drape and curve of a white sheet, the kind that is thrown over dead bodies at a crime scene or in the rubble of a disaster. The craftsmanship is so deft, the lines so realistic—with a slight round jutting of what could be a head here, the protrusion of what might be an elbow there—that as a viewer, it's hard to know whether to marvel over the skill of the artist or to step back, as if one might have unknowingly happened upon some unsafe place.

There are rules for how to behave in the presence of the dead. There are rules for how a body should be treated—think of the truce called at the end of each day's battle on the plains of Troy, men arriving heavy-hearted to retrieve their dead, unafraid of an enemy attack. So too the degradation it was for the body of Hector to be dragged around his city's walls, such probing insult that caused the King to come begging for its return, "Here, I kiss the hands of the man who murdered my son."

Though neither of us says it aloud, I know we are both thinking of Diane, wondering if a sheet covered her, which of her features were still visible, hoping retroactively that her body was treated with some respect.

I find my friend Dave cracked open in my sight, not only in this moment but in his eyes, his emails, his willingness that seems new, the way he speaks about his sister, the care he's exhibiting over his parents. I have never seen him so vulnerable, I did not know he was so strong. Grief makes us plastic where we were once metal, brings tackiness to our joints, evaporates our marrow, unhinges our footing. I have been where he has been but I cannot walk the road for him. I can hardly even walk it *with* him, even if he would let me.

What matters now is that we are both surprised by the Warhols, how much we like them, and that he lingers with me in front of the Rothkos because he knows they are my favorite. I had suspected he would love a particular Rauschenberg, mostly black and vertical, all layered textures of grey and bubble wrap, stenciled graffiti and viscous paint. I suspected he would love it, and he does.

We proceed to dinner, our usual routine, and afterward, on the way back to the car, Dave takes my hand. It is, I think, the first time he's ever done that. Just a hand, I know, but it is an opening, perhaps the same one forged years ago, where Phil and I ventured through pen and paper. Loss is, no doubt, back-breakingly transformative. I cannot take back the person I have become in these years; indeed I do not know who I might be if my father had been present all along.

Phil compares the grieving to a river, *damned to be diverted left or right but never where it flowed before.* In J.K. Rowling's popular Harry Potter series, a thoughtful detail—thestrals, winged creatures that pull the chariots up to the school castle—can only be seen by those who have known death. To the rest of the students, thestrals are invisible, and the chariots appear to drive themselves.

What can be seen and known and said? Here are we who have touched death, wild-eyed, with a newly burnished edge.

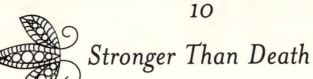

10
Stronger Than Death

Love is at work, it is tireless.
-Paul Éluard

Here are five things I know for certain can be bridged: religion, skin color, age, circumstances of birth and of death.

I was nineteen when Jill and I met. Jill was thirty-nine. My head was shaved as a result of a we're-freshmen-in-college-so-why-the-hell-not moment that my roommate Rebecca and I had experienced. This is why Jill thought that Rebecca and I were Buddhist nuns when we walked into her Introduction to World Religion class; most of the rest of campus assumed that Rebecca and I were dating, but neither of these things were true.

I remember what Jill was wearing the first day I laid eyes on her: a silky blue shell with a blazer, and a long gold necklace with a pendant that looked like an acorn. Ours was not "love at first sight," something I'm not even sure I believe in (of course, we don't have to believe in things for them to exist, do we?) but there *was* something. Enough to make a mental note—*Who is this person?*—and to do my best, among a room of a hundred-plus students, to get her to take notice of me.

She was a teacher crush, I thought. Up to that point in my young life, I had made something of a habit of flirting—more intellectually than sexually, at least on the surface—with people older than me. Teachers, mostly, because they were who I had access to; they were the ones who spoke about things I wanted to know. I was the kind of child who did not fit very well with people her own age.

We only children often feel more comfortable around adults than kids. But my crush on Jill was different, because as it progressed, she did not push me away. As we sat across from each other at her desk during countless office hours, talking or doing our respective work in comfortable silence, it became apparent that she also had a crush on me. Unlike many others who had come before her, she did not renounce our connection or limit it. We were both terrified and exhilarated, but we could not deny what was between us. So we have tried to honor it instead.

Jill was born on July 25th, 1963; John F. Kennedy was the President of the United States. A loaf of bread cost twenty-two cents, just seven cents less than a gallon of gas. Four black girls died in a church bombing in Birmingham, Alabama that year, and on the day of Jill's birth, the United States signed a nuclear test ban treaty. She was born during that same sweltering summer in which Dr. King delivered his "I Have a Dream Speech" on the steps of the Lincoln Memorial. James Meredith graduated from Ole Miss, and The Beatles and Roy Orbison ruled the pop charts. 1963 was the year zip codes were introduced, and *The Beverly Hillbillies* was the number one show on television.

I was born on November 24th, 1982; Ronald Reagan was President. Meryl Streep won an Oscar that year for her role in *Sophie's Choice*, one of Jill's favorite films. *E.T.* was released that year, grossing more money than *Star Wars*. A gallon of gas cost ninety-one cents. The year of my birth ushered in a recession, and The Vietnam Veterans Memorial was dedicated. *TIME'S* "Man of the Year" (you could still use gendered language like that back then) was The Computer. Michael Jackson released *Thriller*, and *Dallas* was the top show on TV.

Jill was born into a white, blue-collar family in Shreveport, Louisiana. Her father was a police officer, her mother a nurse—they met in a hospital emergency room and have been married for fifty-five years. He was born in 1922, she in 1933 and they still fill their deep freezers (yes, plural) as if they are guarding against the Great Depression. As a little girl, Jill learned to help in the garden, shell peas into a grocery sack, stand stock-still while her mother hunted squirrels, and to pray in tongues. Now she is the only person in her family to have earned a Ph. D.

I am the American-born daughter of Indian immigrants, themselves the product of an arranged marriage and the first generation to have come of age in an independent India. They both held Masters degrees and spoke four languages between the two of them. When my father died in 2006, they had been married for almost forty years. When I was a little girl, I attended private school, took piano lessons, played in the backyard, and spent most of my time with books. I'm the only daughter in my parents' group of friends who didn't go to law school or medical school. Oh, and both Jill and I turned out to be gay.

HERS
Folding chairs scrape her aunt's garage floor; as apostles in the book of Acts, it is the believers, not the building, that make a church. The women have tall hair and cat-eye glasses, the men are wearing half-sleeve shirts which smell of cut grass and tobacco. Mother's hand grips her small one tight.

She wasn't allowed to wear her boots today, has been wrangled instead into a dress she hates. This child, blond as a cherub, grave as a stone, unreadable. Someone begins to sing and the small soul is present, firmly here.

MINE
I awaken to the sound of morning prayers in Sanskrit; when she sings, my mother's voice sounds bigger, glorious. Sometimes I rise early, stealing down the hallway from my bedroom, slipping off my

shoes and sidling up next to Mama, to sing along in the places I know by heart, letting her voice carry mine.

The cloth on the altar shines, and the burning ghee, clove-infused water, and smoky incense smell sweet and secret. Mama moves the flame around the images of the gods and goddesses. My favorite is Ganeshji, with his elephant head.

HERS

She is seven years old the first time, in a brush arbor in north Louisiana. Words speed and fall and dance and soar, mean nothing, mean everything. She is open, ready, unafraid. The Spirit of the Lord is here in this place. The Spirit speaks through you. Speak.

MINE

I am eleven years old, in a church basement in Memphis, Tennessee. My people have rented this space on a Saturday to perform Hindu rituals on the linoleum floor. I am dressed in red, all eyes on me. Today I am the vehicle. Today I play the goddess.

HERS

Home to skillets full of cornbread. Home to beans and peas dressed with pork fat, dressing the birds and the deer, trussed up, her little cousin likes to hold the guts. Yard sale china cups full of coffee, guns locked up in a closet, under the bed. There is always something to speak of: the latest fishing lure, Uncle Bob's health, the deck that needs repairing, what a friend we have in Jesus. Welcome to the Carroll family, where the men are men and the women are men, too.

MINE

I slip into a world that the kids at school do not know. Where our parents speak languages we kids do not know. Where everyone is loud and stays up late and pinches you on the cheek. Where I call "Uncle" and "Aunty" people who do not share my blood. Where everyone is brown, and India is nothing to be ashamed of.

HERS

She discovers the drums, begs for lessons. Mother is sharp and defiant when she tells Daddy, "There's no reason she can't play them just because she's a girl." And she's good, so good that soon she is playing with adults, playing at church, two, three, five days a week. Up late at night, listening to records with headphones on, picking out each part, singing the harmonies, rehearsing silently with talented wrists.

MINE

My parents discover their child telling stories, have the foresight to write them down before I can write myself. In a cloth-bound journal with bows on the cover, the pages gradually give way to my own hand, looped cursive becoming teenaged scrawl. This is how I learn to make sense of the world, of myself. One journal becoming two, becoming four, becoming a shelf crammed full of the things a young soul has to say.

HERS

School is not fun, does not come easily. Her parents transfer her away from public school, stretch dollars so that their daughter won't talk "black" anymore, can be properly and proudly educated. She is uncomfortable among the privilege, sticks her tongue out in pictures because she doesn't know what else to do, the quietly earnest class clown. School is what she must endure to get home to her music.

MINE

School is a sanctuary, comes easily. My parents never have to ask if I've done my homework, never once help with an assignment, do not interfere. The classroom is the only place where I feel competent, worthy, since other girls my age do not make sense, do not seem to like me. I gravitate toward teachers, older peers—"You're so mature for your age" becomes my life's exasperating refrain. At lunch I sit alone, write, and read.

OURS

Only daughters of older parents. Fiercely desired pre-utero and guarded since birth by strong, snaking mothers. Fathers are unusually sensitive men, feminists for their time and place, dote on us completely—daddy's girls. We spend a great deal of time alone, learn not to mind. We read. We rarely need to be reminded to obey.

OURS

From our mothers, we were given: iron-clad determination, ambition, and a certain inability to admit when we are wrong. Women who can cook anything and make it good, who do their own yard work, who will impress you because they are not trying to, who are more than a little miffed by the difficulties they've been handed and the seeming luck of everyone else. Who show their love by hounding, fussing, and insisting. Of whom their husbands are a little scared.

OURS

From our fathers, we inherit: charm, the ability to flirt, and a sense of integrity. Men who strike up conversation with strangers, who befriend folks in line at the store, who are not afraid to say "I love you," who give big hugs. Who were raised by sisters, and so do not mind strong-willed women, found two for their wives and then helped raise two more. Who pulled themselves up by their bootstraps. Who show their love by spoiling. Of whom their daughters make heroes.

Things I have learned since I met Jill: how to make pan gravy, what it's like to watch the sun rise over a duck pond, to always save your fry grease in a separate jar for later use, the proper use of the phrase "whoppy-jawed," what a jig head is, how to climb into a pickup truck with a skirt on, what it feels like to shoot a gun, and the goodness of pickled okra.

With me I have brought: trays of spices, a household altar, Tibetan incense, Sanskrit prayers, icons of elephant-headed Ganesh, strange foods she has grown to love, including homemade yogurt rendered tangy and thick, the brown people way, yoga on the living room rug, and dozens of discarded *bindis* littering our bathroom counters.

Within the architecture of every life, there are worlds unknown, expertise and artistry and magic. Bait and spin and tackle. *Aarti* and *puja* and saris. Crack the cumin and cook the *vagar* and pin the pleats and strain the *chai*. Reel and bob and bail and float. Shells and shot and safety and scope. Render the lard and can the tomatoes and cook up a mess o' greens—these wholly "other" languages. What we might not have seen or ever know, what I would never have respected or understood. And what more is left. That is, forever, the question; how much more might we have left?

In fishing terminology, a "floater" drops and maintains your hook at the depth that you are after.

Jill's tumor was discovered when she went to see a doctor for neck pain, the result of a few months' worth of scrubbing paint off of our concrete dining room floor to ready it to be stained and polished in time for our annual party celebrating *Diwali*, the Hindu Festival of Lights. Along with a pinched nerve in her neck, tests and scans showed a shadowy mass in the middle of her sternum, near her heart. After weeks of waiting and more tests, thymoma became the official diagnosis. Extremely rare and slow-growing, a thymoma is a cancer of the thymus, a gland that is active during childhood (producing infection-fighting cells called lymphocytes) but which, in most people, retreats or shrinks as you age. In Jill's case, it did not.

Our relationship with our bodies is quite paradoxical. On the one hand, it hardly gets more intimate than one's own physical habitat; given that we are not quite sure, as humans, how to exist without bodies, you might not be able to call it a relationship at all, but simply a mode of existence. We have no choice but to blow our noses, wipe our bottoms, manage the flow of blood, in and out, to notice changes in weight, in shape. But on the other hand, do we really know much about what is going on in our own bodies at any given time? Headache here, sore spot there, and we may not be able to account for it at all. Billions of processes take place inside of us each day, without us having to authorize or even realize that they are happening. There are whole worlds and battles being fought of which we remain blissfully ignorant—until those processes we are so used to operating smoothly, stop.

I remember watching *Fantastic Voyage* as a girl, a movie in which a submarine and its medical crew are magically shrunk down and injected into the bloodstream of a high-level diplomat who has barely survived an assassination attempt. The film's vintage sixties special effects rendered the imaginary body's interior as if the landscape of a faraway planet—the webbing of tissue became a forest, the craggy walls of an artery suddenly a cavern carved as if out of some great mountain range. The inner space of the body is, in a sense, the real last frontier.

In the most remote region of Antarctica, Lake Vostok sits underneath two-and-a-half miles of solid ice. The lake, which Russian scientists very recently reported they have reached the surface of after decades of drilling, has been isolated from the external world, devoid of sunlight, for approximately twenty million years. Though the temperature down there is -3 degrees C, the enormous pressure exerted by the oppressive ice block above keeps the lake in a liquid

state. Is there life down there? It's possible. Ecosystems can evolve
to exist in the unlikeliest places: microscopic creatures that thrive in
the soil at a volcano's lip or in radioactive pools of liquid.

*"There are more things in Heaven and Earth, Horatio, than are
dreamt of in your philosophy."*
(William Shakespeare, *Hamlet*, Act I, Scene V)

In the city of Amer, in the state of Rajasthan, a dry, mountainous
piece of Northern India, there is a temple set into the foothills which
is dedicated to the goddess Kali. Kali is best known, among her many
epithets, for being the bringer of destruction; she is a fierce warrior
who wears the skulls of men for her necklace, and their severed limbs
as her belt. She is the conflagration of death and disease, the terrifying "Black One," as her name signifies, gruesome, bloody, and wild.
But she is also a metaphorical warrior, destroyer of ignorance and ego.

For Rajasthanis, an affiliation with Kali makes sense; the region
is one of the few that remained under Hindu control throughout
history, fending off takeover by the Muslim Mughals—a bellicose
state deserves a warrior goddess. But statues and wall-hangings of the
goddess are also to be found in the poorest, most lost-in-time villages
in all parts of India. For when all that protects one from sickness
are prayers, and death looms dark over the life of your family, why
not keep the Black One as close as you can? Placate her, sacrifice to
her, watch her out of the corner of one eye.

I have been to the Kali temple in Amer; I have heard the clang-
ing bells that call one to prayer, felt my eyes water with the sting of
incense, watched the offerings line up against the rock wall of the
cave. And I have begged shamelessly, to whatever or whoever might
be listening, that sickness would pass my beloved by. To bargain,
to plead, to trick death or try and put her off of your trail: there is
nothing so human as this.

After Jill's initial chemotherapy consultation with her oncologist, during which we were regaled with pages of drug information, disclaimers, instructions, and possible side effects (one of which is cancer, another of which is death), we began in our house to refer to the chemical cocktail of poison as "Hurricane Kali." "It takes something more toxic than the disease to kill the disease," Jill wrote to our friends in explanation. One of those friends bought Kali necklaces for all of us to wear. We kept an icon of the goddess on our refrigerator. In our family's mythology, Kali the chemical hurricane became our ally, our mercenary, our attempt to grab onto the swirling forces of death, our emissary into the dark, unknowable world of Jill's body.

M.D. Anderson Cancer Center, 5:15 a.m.

I can't even remember what floor we're on, how we got here this morning, which elevators we came in through the lobby. To be separated from Jill makes my mind fuzzy and my stomach knotty, as if our connection, our partnership, our relationship is experiencing static because one side of the pair is missing, unconscious, temporarily gone.

I have noticed that my eighth grade students, when they have the chance to write on something—a white board, a piece of blank paper, a bathroom stall—almost always revert to some version of "X WAS HERE." I want to dig through my bag for a Sharpie and write on the walls of this waiting room "I WAS HERE." I have done this. I have waited. I have sat in this limbo. I have breathed this hospital air.

A conversation with a college friend of mine has stuck in my mind; she is now a doctor, the emergency kind, who travels to Guatemala to do medical volunteer work for a few weeks at a time. The contrast in resources is so obscene that young, American doctors are forced to completely shift their thinking. Here, within the American medical system, as screwed up as it is, doctors operate under the premise that running every possible test, doing every possible procedure, cataloguing a complete genealogy of a problem, and crossing things out by process of elimination is the proper way of doing things. All Hail the land of plenty, gleaming white hospitals with their science and their ability to fix things.

But when there is no gleaming white, no money, and no means of performing test after test, what is best practice? What *is* medicine? My friend recounts: "Do I tell a man to take two days off of work and travel to the nearest city to have an expensive test, which will cost him two months' salary and most likely confirm what I suspect? And then when my diagnosis is confirmed, what treatment options will be available to this man? He can't afford the drugs he needs. He will die soon. So I give him Advil and tell him to go be with his family." There is "doctor" the noun, and then there is "doctor" the verb: to alter, disguise, falsify.

It seems to me that there are now so many particulars, so many millions of variations on the human experience, that it hardly seems right to talk about "us" as if we are some kind of godforsaken family. When a five-dollar mosquito net could protect the lives of entire family halfway across the globe, and I spend that much on my morning coffee, does it really matter if the babies all babble and coo the same?

I can now add to the list of things I've done: graded papers in a chemo room, flushed a PICC line dozens of times, shaved my spouse's head, cleaned her up after she was unable to make to the bathroom in time and was too worn out from surgery to clean herself.

This is the bargain we are all supposed to accept: you will learn to love something, and then it will die. If the purpose of this life is to keep our egos in manageable enough balance so that we can both make ourselves vulnerable enough to love and form human connection so we aren't total assholes all of the time, and to maintain enough sense of ourselves that we do some good in the world and don't all say "the hell with it" and wander off into the forest, then I think, *Who would set things up like this?* Or worse, who would *sign up* for this? Well, I guess I would.

Kali did what we asked her, but she did more, too; she demolished a good bit of illusion and ego, along with a tumor. One's sense of what's real, what matters, one's place in the scheme of things, cancer and Kali will recalibrate all of that. And they will leave a six-inch scar behind.

Our first post-cancer trip was to a wedding, where I was a bridesmaid and Jill sat in a pew with two months' worth of regrown hair atop her head, looking much like I had on the day we first met. Though the wedding was not ours, the words "in sickness and in health" rang inside the stained-glass church with new meaning. I was asked to give one of the readings, from the Song of Solomon, which almost took my breath with its aptness: *Set thyself as a seal upon my heart, for love is stronger than death, passion fiercer than the grave.*

And the congregation replied, "Amen."

Months later, our dog is back from a dental surgery, woozy and disoriented from drugs. My heart is bruised to see her this vulnerable, reminding me that she is already a pretty old bag of bones. "One of us will have to do this for the other someday," I say to Jill as I hold the dog's trembling body, and though it's simply the truth that I've spoken, something tears the air. Later that night, we are tangled in bed—making noise, making love, making sure to pin ourselves to each other for as long as we can. We have cheated death for now, but not forever. Drop the floater, and hold.

11

River of Language

It is religion that carries language. The river of language is God.
-Don DeLillo

Before we left for India, my mother gave me a present: a digital voice recorder, light as travel-sized pack of tissues and about the length of a deck of cards. It became my tricky little bug, easily hidden instrument of preservation. I felt like a kid with a Mason jar trying to catch the air of a magical place, close the lid on it, and carry it with me someplace else, collecting conversations and sounds I was afraid I would forget. If I managed to jar the noise of India, I thought I might keep it with me forever.

TRACK ONE: JUHU BEACH

My own voice announces the time—6:45 a.m.—as the sound of the waves and the wind pour in. I can just make out my uncle's and father's voices, their inflections familiar even if I cannot distinguish individual words. I walk in the other direction, closer to the water.

Earlier, as we parked in the nearby public lot, I noticed decorative tiles interspersed among the rough stone. Depicted on the three just beyond our car were Hanuman, the Hindu messenger god, the Buddha in seated meditation, and Jesus, affixed to the cross and attended by two disciples.

India is not afraid of religion. India wears its beliefs—plural—on its sleeve, folds its icons and deities into the thousands-of-years-old mix, fills the air with prayers and invocations in dozens of languages.

Kipling got at least one thing right when he said, "All India is full of holy men stammering gospels in strange tongues; shaken and consumed in the fires of their own zeal; dreamers, babblers, and visionaries: as it has been from the beginning and will continue to the end."

TRACK TWO: MUZZEIN'S CALL

When I was twelve years old, I heard the Muslim call to prayer for the first time. We were in India, driving home from the beach at sunset, just before the evening crowds arrived, and the windows of our taxi were rolled down halfway, as this was long before they were air-conditioned as they are now. From my place in the backseat, I held a view to the south, out towards the water. With the sun blazing orange above the horizon, everything within my view appeared in a silhouette of black, the water shimmering from behind. At the very edge of the shore stretched a moving line of human figures, perhaps a quarter-mile long, making their way across a land bridge which the tide had recently pulled back to reveal. A sound, what I now know to be the *muezzin's* call, came clear across traffic and in through our car window. This voice, male, was full of dips and curves, distinctive and unhurried. Though I had never heard the sound before, melody of worship was familiar to me, even if this particular tongue was not.

I knew, instinctively, what was drawing those people across that narrow strip of land, much better than I knew the details of evening prayers at Muslim mosques. It seemed to me the most obvious thing in the world, that a voice should come from the sky to call men and women to worship. When I returned to India as an adult, I recorded the sound of the *muzzein* from my uncle's balcony twice, just barely able to pick it out of the cacophony of other sounds in the air: horns honking, bicycle bells trilling, vendors calling out their wares, birds squawking from the trees.

In Don DeLillo's novel *The Names*, which plays brilliantly with language, religion, expression, and memory, two hardened men-of-the-world are discussing the Muslim pilgrimage known as the *hajj*, and the ecstatic circling of the black shrine called the *Ka'baa*, which is the culmination of three days of ritual observance.

"Would you?" one man asks the other.

"To honor God?" his companion says in reply.

"Yes, I would run."

TRACK THREE: MAHALAXMI TEMPLE

In the late 1700s, William Hornby, governor of what was then called Bombay, planned an insanely ambitious civil engineering project to create a single landmass from the seven islands which originally constituted the city. Though full of foresight, Horby's brainchild and its proposed costs were deemed extravagant and summarily rejected by the higher-ups at the East India Company. He proceeded as planned anyway. All was going well until a fortification wall constructed near the coastline began to collapse. It was rebuilt, stronger, thicker, but high tides pushed it down again. This failure, coupled with the lack of official support and funding, stirred up dissent and abandonment of the project seemed imminent.

Just so, one of the project's chief engineers had a dream. In this dream, the goddess Lakshmi appeared in all her splendor and with instructions: *Search the seabed*, she told the sleeping man, *and there you will find three statues. One is a likeness of me, the other two are of my sisters, Kali and Saraswati. Bring them to the surface, house them in a worthy way, and your third-built wall will stand.* And so the Mahalaxmi Temple was built, and so the Hornby Vellard still stands against the sea.

We build beautiful monuments because we believe crazy things. Because we do not believe that our hearts are enough of an offering.

My memories of the Mahalaxmi temple are double, one from an early visit at one at age twelve, the second at age twenty-three, when

I recorded the noise of the worshippers around me. The first time, wearing unfortunate glasses, sporting a poufy, too-adult hairdo, standing in front of the temple's entrance, holding a tray full of offerings, bananas, mangoes, almonds, cashews, a small tumble of rock-candy nuggets. As a grown woman, I went through the same motions, everything looking much smaller than I remembered it, awkward and mostly unimpressive. A long sidewalk leads up to the temple steps and small stalls crowded along either side transition from secular to sacred. Farthest away from the temple, the goods are akin to a gas station's spread, cold drinks and disposable cameras, gum and cigarettes. As you walk closer, these un-holy things make way for the bright *accoutrement* of my religion's choosing: garlands of fresh flowers, stainless-steel *thallis* lined with Indian fabric, chunks of camphor, coins, fruits like coconut, mango, papaya, and banana, sweets made out of nuts or chickpea flower, the fancier ones topped with pieces of edible silver and gold leaf. When I stopped with my parents to buy an offering, I left my shoes behind with the stall's owner and realized how soft my American feet were against the hot concrete.

I was raised to see my tradition through Western eyes, but also knew that I was supposed to remain loyal to it even while passing among the white kids. It is a contradictory prospect, to be raised both inside of something and in opposition to it. Contradictory and confusing, and not without shame. At school and almost everywhere else, the straight, upward line of history taken to be the truth, the omnipresent "progress," transparent to me until I realized that I, at times, looked on my own religion as primitive and ridiculous in comparison to the "civilized" rituals of the Christianity that surrounded me. And then, ironically, it was white professors in college who introduced me to my own people's conceptualization of time as a circle, circles within circles, spinning in infinity, *hallelujah*.

At the temple, I still feel reverent, if out of nothing more than habit or in respect and deference to the mantras being recited under the breath of folks all around me. I make my way in line up to the priest, hand him my *thalli* to be blessed, receive the vermillion mark of *tikka* on my forehead. I bow my head, close my eyes. If there is something here, I will honor it.

Exiting the women's side, a path leads to the back of the temple and then on to several smaller shrines featuring other gods: Ganesh, Shiva, even an imprint of the Buddha's feet as he is often incorporated back into the Hindu pantheon from which he was generated. Behind all this is water, the Indian Ocean, blue and frothy below the cliff on which the temple was built.

My father walks over with a newspaper cone full of roasted garbanzo beans, *channa*, spiced and salted by a nearby vendor. I pour some into my palm, throw the handful back into my mouth just as he does. In moments like these, it is almost as if I am playing a role, Nishta the Indian girl. Nishta who feels good in bare feet and a covered head. Nishta who wears Indian clothes comfortably, the standard *salwar kameez*, loose pants and a long tunic top with a scarf for decoration and modesty's sake. Nishta who defers to her parents, reads quietly in the corner of the room, takes notes on conversations she overhears, scoops up *sabjis* with a corner of *parantha* in her right hand, takes her milky tea Indian style, half-a-dozen-times-a-day.

We walk back down the temple steps and to the stall where we left our shoes. My father calls our driver on the Indian cell phone he borrowed from relatives, and while we wait for the car to arrive, my mother buys jasmine for my hair, fifty blooms all strung together by an old widow in a white sari. "It's like having your own portable perfume all day," Mama says as she affixes it to my half-ponytail. I ask her to take a picture, me standing in sunglasses with a close-mouthed smile and a Pepsi sign in the background. My *salwar kameeze* is periwinkle blue; in the photograph we later get developed, my scarf is draped around my shoulders, dipping into a "U" shape in the front. I'm wearing a silver-and-pearl necklace my parents had just bought for me and there is a look on my face even I can't quite place. When I look at it now, I understand why cameras once were thought to be mechanisms of witchcraft, as if they could capture a piece of you, your soul.

TRACK FOUR: BALCONY

The city at night, going about its business. Mumbai is a crush of people of all kinds: beggars, businessmen, small families perched impossibly on narrow scooters, wealthy expatriates who have settled in the tropical clime, men and women from various other Indian states who speak dozens of mother tongues, rug weavers, shoe shiners, politicians, protestors, cab drivers, holy men, teachers, artists, street performers with trained monkeys.

For an American, India is overwhelming at first—scary, even. We Westerners are committed to our individuality and distinctness, unwilling to give into the idea that we are but one in a crowd of many. In India, it's nearly impossible to live your life in particular; you are forced to live it in common. You are among the mass of humanity, swept up in a sea of worry and doubt and trouble and belief.

Hinduism is famous for its teaching that there are many paths up the same mountain, many ways to live a righteous life and honor God. Regardless of your occupation--whether you are a humble potter or a righteous holy man--my religion asserts that if you live and act with a right heart, you are on the right track. As it says in the *Bhagavad Gita*, "Any man who acts with honor cannot go the wrong way."

TRACK FIVE: HARIMANDIR SAHIB

In my father's home state of Amritsar, I ride with my parents to the Pakistani border and back, watching the countryside, life there still so provincial: brick-bakers and farmers, slow and easy water buffaloes. We stop to buy bottled water and stand in the sun. No one in the entire world except my parents knows where I am in this moment.

We decide to skip the border-closing ceremony on the advice of our cab driver, who swears it isn't all that exiting or worth the wait, and advises us to head to the Golden Temple, Sikhism's holy shrine before darkness falls. There will be light still for me to take pictures, but the day's heat will have withdrawn, and I'll be able to catch the evening recitations and chants on my little magic device.

We go back to our hotel so that I can prepare myself, wash my hair and put on a new *salwar kameez*; true, we were created, sweat and all, but there is something to being clean, prepared, washed. Beauty can happen anywhere; one's body is not a bad place to start.

As a kid, I was uncertain around those my own age. When, at dinner parties, it was customary for the kids to separate off from the adults at dinner parties—upstairs to watch television, a movie or play Nintendo (all foreign goods for me who grew up without cable or video games, watched mostly PBS and Disney movies)—often enough, I would sit in a corner by myself with a book I had brought, or huddle next to my mom and listen quietly to the adults talk. These choices I made mostly out of a deep sense of discomfort, a knowing that I was not "cool" and a feeling that I couldn't really hold my own with those who were. Being a goody-two-shoes was a way to hide from the other kids who scared me. Better to stick with the adults, where my difference was praised, where my parents would receive compliments for having such a thoughtful, well-behaved child.

But at the *kirtans*--music parties--we attended, I chose to sit with my mom for a different reason; I wanted to listen. I was a child predisposed for the sacred; I knew how to be still. Sikhs sing from their holy book, the *Guru Granth Sahib,* in Punjabi, a language my parents understood. Someone would coax notes out of the *harmonium,* an instrument I love because it is so distinctive that it immediately identifies that its music belongs to my people. Other uncles would play the *tablas*--hand drums--and then the singing would begin.

When I was little, I didn't realize—I know it sounds implausible, but it's true—I didn't know that these people belonged to a different religion from us. My parents' Indian friends were all from different states and regions, spoke different languages (for many of them, their common tongue was English), and had unusual customs that my nuclear family didn't share. It wasn't until I became a religious studies major in college that I put the pieces together, studying Sikhism on paper, taking down the notes—oh! *That's* what that was. I like to think it was a testament, my ignorance, to the environment I grew up in. My parents did not draw thick boundary lines as far as belief and worship were concerned. My father, though raised Hindu, visited the Golden Temple as a kid with his friends who were Sikh. "There was never anyone who said we shouldn't go," he tells me on the recording, "that this wasn't for Hindus. As far as we knew, it was a holy place for us, too." There was so much that was fair game.

For a golden building, there is nothing garish about the Golden Temple. Perhaps it was the dimming dusk light that tempered the marble so perfectly, but I found each moment of that walk around the temple so rightly placed that the essence of it seemed pure and true. What I love about the Sikhs is the honor they hold so dear, a sense of propriety not just for propriety's sake, but something deeper. In their highest expression, they are about feeding the poor, affirming the power of words, radical gender equity, and coming to the aid of the defenseless. And they honor, above any saint or holy man, a book.

My parents and I walked through the building and sat around the reflecting pool for over an hour, our heads covered, our feet barefoot and washed, all the while with the sound of the stylized, musical reading being broadcast throughout the complex. On the recording, you can hear the sound of drums and babies crying in the background as the assembled crowd recites the prayers that will put their holy book to bed for the night.

Our worship is imperfect, but it is ours.

TRACK SIX: BELLS

Hanuman is Hinduism's messenger god, known for his selfless and heroic acts, particularly in devotion to Lord Rama. My favorite story about Hanuman comes from the *Ramanaya*, the ancient tale that recounts the story of Lord Rama's fight against the evil demon Ravana. At one point in the truly epic battle, Rama's brother is severely wounded, and Hanuman is sent to fetch a life-restoring herb, called *sanjivani*, from the Himalayas. Hanuman, who has the gift of flight, travels across the sky to the mountains to search for the herb, but finds that he is unable to identify it. Unwilling to risk choosing the wrong plant, Hanuman simply pulls off a mountain top, the crater dangling roots, its plants shivering in the wind, and delivers it to Rama.

It was a humble Hanuman temple at which my father worshipped as a boy. Though it has now been replaced by a bigger, fancier building, priests and their young apprentices still honor Hanuman in a humbler way, in a grove of trees nearby. I made a recording of the music they made, a louder, more brusque version of church handbells, ringing out among the trees and to the heavens.

We are moved to make noise, make our presence known, assert our selfhood as if tossing ourselves like dice. We are compelled to celebrate and praise, even if we don't know exactly what we are praising or celebrating. It doesn't take much; just some men, robed in orange and ringing bells with all their might.

TRACK SEVEN: WORLD RELIGIONS DAY

In New Delhi, my parents and I spend a day on our own veritable World Religions tour, making the religious studies major in me very happy. We start with a North Indian style Hindu temple, its statuary stunning in the half-light, then move to a Sikh *gurdwara*, with its distinctive mushrooming tower, followed by a dazzlingly marble-white and bejeweled Jain temple, touch the pillar of *Alai Darwaza*, a famous Muslim monument ringed in giant Arabic inscriptions carved in relief, then stop by a Baha'i meditation center which looks like a lotus from the distance, and end the day at *Raj Ghat*, where Gandhi's ashes are interred below giant plumeria large enough to climb.

It is fashionable to berate religion in this day and age, in a cynical, post-modern, Western context. Within that view, religion is, at best, an old-fashioned relic, and at worst, an agent of evil. To profess a belief in, or even respect for, religion means you must be an ignorant, backwards person with no regard for science and no tolerance for the differences of others. From this perspective, religion is a force to fear, to contain, to protect innocents from. It is a backwards-looking crutch that humans will hopefully outgrow.

Human beings have done their very worst in the name of religion, this is true. I do not deny that religion *is* often used as a crutch, a system exploited for human gain. After all, whether or not there exists some Divine Being for whose benefit (or to whose horror) all this fuss is being made, it is humans who build—and maintain— religion. Our nature is reflected in its contradictions; its flaws and shortcomings are ours. Therefore it reflects our very worst, and our very best. Because what those critics of religion often fail to point out is that human beings have done and do some of their very best in the name of religion, too: the clinic next to the Hindu temple that is offering free tests for the HIV virus, the *langar* room at the *gurdwara* where free meals are given to those in need, and nonviolent doctrines within Jainism that inspired Gandhi, and, in turn, Martin Luther King, Jr.

TRACK EIGHT: AGRA

We take a trip to Agra to see, of course, the Taj Mahal. The driver drops us off at the train station in Delhi very early in the morning. "This is how the other half travels," my parents tell me, and I can see what they mean. The platforms are crowded, so tightly packed and frantic that you are amazed to find, in the middle of one, an entire family sleeping on their luggage. This is the part of India, I can guess, that looks very much the same as it did forty years ago.

The part of India that comes to American minds when they think of this country: dirty, crowded, smelly, hot.

Our train car is air-conditioned; we can afford it. The travel time is ninety minutes one-way, and so I settle in next to the window with my journal. Outside, rural life flashes by, the regular noise of the wheel-tracks contributing to the exoticism that makes me feel like I'm in a movie. Cows, clusters of buildings, morning fires, men squatting to take a shit by the railroad tracks.

To see the Taj Mahal, you must first line up outside an outer gate, where monkeys taunt tourists from the ramparts. You must pass through a metal detector and into a garden complex, which is lovely but does not belie what's ahead. You take pictures of the red walls, ornamented with inlaid Arabic calligraphy, but do not rush yourself toward the gate that will offer you your first view of the famous monument. You are afraid to see it too quickly, afraid that it will not live up to its reputation, that if you look at it straight-on, it might disappear.

It is stunning, that goes without saying, iconic and luminous and cool to the touch. Many better-informed scholars of art history and religion have written treatises about what makes a structure sacred or beautiful; my own theory is more romantic, something to do with the frenzy of grief and the freedom of absolute power. After all, to whom does the credit for a place like this go? Marble hauled on backs, carvers, masons, calligraphers, elephants, architects, over-worked miners of semi-precious stone. So much of what we value about human culture now are things that we did before we knew better.

In the afternoon, we visit Fatepur Sikri, palace complex of the great king Akbar. Our driver connects us with an old, toothless tour guide who only speaks Urdu, which my mother understands. While he doesn't look like much, it turns out this man can weave an unbelievable story, knows the secrets of this place; my mother translates his words for me and my father. Our guide walks us through the long-abandoned palace rooms, pointing out intricate carvings and weathered frescos. "The British may have stripped the cream off of the top of this place," he tells my mother, referring to the looting done by colonists long ago, "But they could not take away the essential beauty. That still remains today."

They say that Akbar—who lived from 1542-1605 and took for himself three wives, each from a different religion: Islam, Hinduism, & Christianity—had a beautiful singing voice. They say that he would stand on the observation deck that he had built for his Hindu and Muslim wives, so that they might watch for the moon during their respective periods of fasting, and sing. They say that, during periods of draught and famine among his people, Akbar would stand on the platform and sing to call down the rain.

Akbar's court was famous for welcoming Hindu and Muslim musicians alike, a period of mingling that wound up being essential for the development of distinctly Indian music and poetry. But his doctrine of *sulh-i kul*, or absolute peace, came into existence only after a period of intolerance after which Akbar himself admitted to regretting forcing Hindus to convert to Islam at the point of a sword.

Contained within the complex of Fatepur Sikri is the tomb of Salim Chisti, a saint from the Sufi Muslim tradition. Sufis are the mystics within Islam, the poets and whirling dervishes who seek direct, ecstatic connection with God. At the tomb, considered sacred by Muslims and Hindus alike, visitors wait in line to tie a thread to the marble lattice that backs the tomb, linking a prayer to their thread and asking the saint to answer. To ask, to seek, to beg—we do these very human things by default, fruitless and vain though they may be. Because even though we have science, and even though we have medicine, we are still left with our very human, very unchanging condition. The people we love grow sick, and will die.

The wicked are not always punished. We still seek to know what we might be on this planet for.

My favorite Sufi, the thirteenth-century poet Rumi, says "You are the soul and medicine for what wounds the soul."

BONUS TRACK: CAB RADIO
And the songless through him burst into melody.
-said of the Muslim philosopher al-Ghazali

I grew up swimming in the music of the Indian subcontinent—sacred, secular, Hindu, Muslim, Sikh—it mattered not to my father, as long as there was a melody he could hum or sing along to. On weekend afternoons, following luxurious naps, the sound of his music would swell from behind the closed door of my parents' bathroom, the muffled reverberation of my father's magical voice emanating, too, singing along while he took his bath.

He also sang in public: at dinner parties after the food had been served and the chai had been made, at sacred gatherings and secular alike, devotional music and film songs, memorizing music in other languages to perform at the weddings of friends. His voice is one of the things he's most remembered for, one of the things most missed. Lovely, lilting, he could convey very delicate phrasing; his delivery was incredibly sensitive. Never formally trained, simply self-taught, the sound of that voice is what I am most afraid to lose the memory of, the part of him that somehow seems the most essential.

On weekends now myself, I employ the miracle of internet radio to conjure up the songs my father loved most, the men whose talents he admired: Ghulam Ali, Manna Dey, Mohammad Rafi, Jagjit Singh, Nusrat Fateh Ali Khan. Their *bhajans* (Hindu devotional songs), *qawalis* (Sufi devotional songs), and *ghazals* (love songs both secular and sacred) fill my kitchen as I cook, or my office as I write. I praise what he praised. I sing what he sang.

In an unspecified cab ride at some point during our India trip, an old film song came on over the radio: high-pitched female voice, unrushed and mellow. Both of my parents began to sing along, their voices blending smoothly after decades of practice. It was not the first time I had heard them sing together, nor did I know it would be the last. Still, I pressed "record." For those forty-four seconds, I give my whole self in gratitude. A worthy bargain.

Vehicles of Light

"You are looking outwards, and of all things that is what you must now not do. Nobody can advice [sic] and help you, nobody. There is only one single means. Go inside yourself...This before all: ask yourself in the quietest hour of your night: must I write? Dig down into yourself for a deep answer. And if this should be in the affirmative, if you meet this solemn question with a strong and simple "I must," then build your life according to this necessity."

        -Rainer Maria Rilke, *Letters to a Young Poet*

I have kept a journal since I was old enough to write. Actually, I have kept a journal longer than that, because the very first entries in my very first journal, cloth-bound with bow-patterned fabric, are in my parents' handwriting. They took down my dictation of running commentary and rhymes until my own uneven handwriting emerged and I began to record my own stories and poems. Since then, I have accumulated a collection of over thirty journals, in all shapes and sizes and levels of ornamentation and practicality, pages filled with daily minutiae, big questions, tremendous joy, private embarrassments, potent observations, and deep, driving desire.

  I have never *not* written. I have never *not* felt compelled to write. But it took me years and years to figure out why, to be able to explain what I wrote *for*.

In the sixth grade, I was given my very own copy of Edith Hamilton's *Mythology*, with its ancient heroes and heroines, tales of journeys and metamorphoses. Though no one ever said so, I got the sense that this was the first *real* piece of literature we had been given—not a kiddie text with clear moral lessons and a straightforward plot. Instead, it was solid, like the Bible (the only other grownup text we had been permitted at school up to that point), and it was old. And its stories were magical and wild.

These two classics, *Mythology* and the Bible are so widely and routinely taught that adults seem to forget their power when handing them to kids, seem to forget that their tales are fraught, morally ambiguous, and often terrifying. This is, of course, what makes them stunning: think of Orpheus, think of Jesus, two god-like men, passionate and doomed. Death is devastating, but it is also beautiful, which is why, as a sixth grade girl, I was captivated by Orpheus, the golden-haired and honey-voiced boy who charmed the creatures of the forest and field, whose song compelled oak trees to lift their roots and fashion feet, to follow him down to the sea. Brave Orpheus who calmed the rough-and-tumble men of Jason's Argonaut, foiled the Sirens' song, and captured my heart.

Then Orpheus took a wife, beautiful Eurydice, and the two of them were married, only to have the happiest day of their lives ruined when a snake coiled down out of nowhere and bit the bride her on her lovely neck. You know how the rest goes. Eurydice is dragged down to the Underworld; Orpheus, wild with grief, follows. With his cadence and harmonies and perfect pitch, the musician works the impossible, soothing the triple-headed guard dog Cerberus, and gaining passage into the world of the dead. He then proceeds to charm the stone-cold monarchs of this inscrutable land, Hades and his timeshare wife, Persephone, with his song, persuading the two to agree to a bargain.

Eurydice will be brought forth. She will follow behind Orpheus as he plays his music and will journey with him up through the dirt, though she will not be able to speak until they have reached the open air. If they make it, she will be restored to her life to live it out fully. *However* (there's always a "however" in these kinds of stories), Orpheus is not allowed to turn around and look at his newly dead wife, to check for her presence, to ensure that she is following him, that the gods are not simply playing some evil trick on him, as they are wont to toy with mortals for sport. If Orpheus turns his head even an inch before they reach the surface, Eurydice will be permanently reclaimed by death.

Which is exactly what happens. At the first glimpse of sunlight, our hero forgets himself, turns, and sees Eurydice again just long enough to memorize her features saying "Farewell!" before she is pulled back into death forever. He wails, he cries out. I remember I cried, too. I remember telling myself, *I could have done it.* Oh Orpheus of little faith. He tries again but to no avail; the boatman won't even row him across the Styx this time. My musician, stuck, and very much alone.

Do we choose what attracts us, or do we stumble upon it by accident? Faces, bodies, paintings, poems. Goethe and his Faust. Calder and his mobiles. Jesus and his sinners. The Buddha and his tree. We learn, we watch, we wait. We cannot be certain if our mind's interests will cohere. But we try and trust that each accumulates some dose of magic.

In the spring of 2010, I read the *New York Times* review of a new play called *Red*, a two-man show about Mark Rothko and his fictionalized assistant, set during the late part of Rothko's working life. Within a week, I had purchased a ticket to see the show on Broadway, and a plane ticket to take me there. On the same Sunday afternoon that the play won a Tony Award for Best New Play, I sat in the front row, less than three feet away from Alfred Molina as he embodied Rothko, spitting and fuming and philosophizing and occasionally painting.

I fell in love with Rothko like I did Orpheus, though the former is a far less romantic figure than the latter—nowhere near as handsome, but equally as doomed. When I saw one of his famous "color field" paintings for the first time, something about it made sense in a way that most other visual art, to me, had not. I had found plenty of other things beautiful, and could admire them for their technical skill, but they seemed merely ornamental, lacked a certain depth I craved. But when I encountered Rothko, I thought, *This is a grownup painting*, much in the same way that the Bible and Greek mythology had seemed to me to be grownup stories.

I did what all good writers do when they become obsessed with something—I read everything I could get my hands on, without having any idea where or how or even if Rothko fit into the curio cabinet of things in my mind. Like the cocky hero, stupidly proceeding down into the belly of an idea because I couldn't *not*.

I soon learned that Rothko was a meticulous, painstaking, and demanding man. An ardent opera fan with special fondness for Mozart's masterpieces *Don Giovanni* and *The Magic Flute*, Rothko saw his role as a painter as akin to that of a composer's, bringing each of his paintings into the world like characters in an ensemble. Here the lovely heroine, here the dashing prince, the evil queen, the drunken sidekick, the mysterious priest. Both the composer and the painter must find the harmonies, the proper placement, imbue the spectacle with substance. And Rothko was not only the composer but the producer, director, and stage manager of his own work, exacting and relentless.

Rebecca and I met when we were assigned to the same dorm room as freshman at Rice University in Houston, Texas. Within a few months, we were fast friends and had pledged to each other, in the earnest but no less powerful way that only twenty year-olds can, that we would pursue our art (hers visual, mine written) vigorously, without waiting for a mid-life crisis to spur us to act.

When you are young and wish to be an artist, you have to figure out what "being an artist" actually means. Do you have to be melodramatic and tortured, or can you be a good person and make good art at the same time? Do you need formal training or will it destroy whatever talent you already have? Should you do art "on the side" or try and make it your career?

To feel compelled to make art is one thing: to actually make it is another.

After Ovid and Edith Hamilton who translated him, Rainer Maria Rilke's version of the Orpheus story is surely the most widely read. Rilke tells his version in fifty-five sonnets, conceived, if we are to believe his own accounts, in a frenzied burst of inspiration. "I birthed the poems whole," he said, delivering them one after the other in the course of a mere two weeks in February of 1922.

Sonnets to Orpheus was the first thing he had written in years. He spent a long time wandering Europe post-World War One, and afterwards he picked up the very same stories of Ovid's that I would encounter some seventy years later in the second-story classroom of an all-girls prep school in Tennessee. Then somebody died, as people do—Vera Knoop, a nineteen-year-old dancer who been a girlhood playmate of Rilke's daughter—and this loss of someone young and beautiful set Rilke to thinking about Eurydice.

Finally, one last addition to the curio cabinet of the poet's mind; Baladine Klossowska, his mistress at the time, is said to have tacked a postcard to the wall above the poet's desk during one of her visits, a pen-and-ink drawing of Orpheus the musician, taming the beasts of the field. Soon after, Rilke became his own Orpheus, chasing his memory of Vera into the Underworld the way Eurydice herself was pursued.

I do not wish to imply that the existence of an artistic master-piece like the *Sonnets* can be fully accounted for by biographical cause-and-effect. Indeed, Rilke's own description of his experience writing the *Sonnets* sounds (to the religious studies major in me) more akin to prophecy than anything else; the prophet hears a voice and becomes the messenger, a vessel. Rilke insisted that he did not create the *Sonnets*, rather that he transcribed them. He referred to the experience as "a single, breathless act of obedience."

Toward the end of his life, Rothko sought the opportunity to create paintings that would hang somewhere pure—not a restaurant or a museum, but a temple of sorts, a theatre of art, a stage, a sacred place. Not remotely a religious man and a fond reader of Nietzsche, Rothko was very clear that he did not want some kind of cutesy, comforting space. He wanted to create an experience, and a confrontational one at that, a building in which viewers would be forced to deal with the art in front of them.

For Rothko, art was not *about* experience; it *was* experience. He used the word *ineluctable*— "not to be resisted." A painting must interrogate its viewer. And viewers were not just floating eyes but whole, embodied beings. That is why Rothko's famous color field paintings are so large; by painting on canvasses taller and wider than the human body, Rothko sought to place his viewers *inside* his paintings. He wanted them to feel enveloped in intimate space. Patches of yellows and reds, greens and blues, blurring their edges as if inviting one in.

Luckily for Rothko, his desire to build a magnum opus was matched by the sponsorship of John and Dominque de Menil, well-known patrons of the Modern Art movement and heirs to a large Texas oil fortune. The couple commissioned Rothko to design a non-denominational chapel on the grounds of St. Thomas University in Houston, promising that his paintings would be the only aesthetic feature allowed in the chapel, save natural light. Then they let the artist go.

The Rothko Chapel is tucked away inside a fine, grassy neighborhood at the heart of Houston's city center. Within walking distance of the chapel: El Pueblito, a mediocre Mexican restaurant with a fabulous patio, Lucky Burger, which serves hamburgers and greasy Chinese food, La Colombe D'or, where jackets are required for expensive French food, Alabama Ice House, where bikers go for afternoon beers, and 1601 Colquitt, the sprawling rental house where I lived with Rebecca during my senior year of college. We took advantage of our prime location, walking from the Colquitt house to the now defunct Café Artiste in our pajamas for Sunday brunch, biking to Rice University's campus for work and classes, and frequently occupying the Rothko Chapel's grassy grounds and quiet interior.

It was when we were living in this neighborhood that Rebecca's mom was diagnosed with cancer: a uterine mass discovered during a routine gynecological exam. Given her age and family history, surgery was performed a week later. Surgeons took out not only her uterus, but her ovaries, cervix, and appendix as well. Chemotherapy commenced.

From the outside, the chapel doesn't look like much. An octagon of creamy brick, the building seems almost an afterthought to the manicured lawn, sheltering oaks, and reflecting pool that surround it. The chapel has no windows, only skylights, as Rothko demanded. Heavy metal doors keep the trafficking of light and humans well-regulated. A volunteer receptionist sits at a desk that dominates the lobby, which is about the size of a freight elevator. She will ask for your signature and hometown, point you towards pamphlets and brochures, and invite you to sign the guestbook on your way out. Pushed up against the glass walls of the reception area are low wooden benches stacked with copies of assorted sacred texts from the world's religions.

Scaling in the Rothko Chapel installation is, of course, deliberate. Rothko left no room for compartmentalizing his composition. Its elements cannot be broken down to more comfortably fit the human scale. Like the classical Greek precedents that inspired him, Rothko's panels are designed to both diminish and uplift their embodied viewer. Man's place in the world, at once central and insignificant. In Latin: *Deus absconditus*. God is hidden, if not altogether missing.

Rebecca's mother, Karen, was a Latin teacher. Filled to the brim with an unbridled goodness and enthusiasm that only PBS television characters seem to have, she was the kind of woman whom it would be impossible to embarrass. She invented dozens of goofy songs to teach her students Latin grammar; she mailed Rebecca and me homemade Valentines every year; she picked and dried her own lavender; she had the most fabulous smile.

Karen was a believer. While the Taliban occupied Afghanistan and were committing astounding human and civil rights abuses, parading around in old Soviet tanks, brandishing machine guns, Karen wrote them a letter. With every earnestness, she commended those masked Muslim extremists to the God in whom she trusted that both she and they believed. She sent her letter to the United States ambassador for Afghanistan, asking him to forward it on her behalf.

Maybe it helps to know that Karen belonged the Church of Christ, the kind that does not sing along with instruments or baptize with just a sprinkling. She converted as an adult, after marrying young and participating in the usual, mildly scandalous things that college students do. But in the Church of Christ, you have to be willing to sign your life beside that Protestant creed, *sola scriptura*. You have to learn to lift your voice, listen for the harmonies, join an unaccompanied chorus. And like Jesus, upon whom the dove descended at the River Jordan, you must choose to be immersed. Any body of water will do, as long as you go all in.

I lost my father first; no one was expecting that. Karen had been fighting cancer for almost two years the summer my father found himself gasping for breath after climbing the stairs to go to bed. He went to see his primary care doctor who sent him to a specialist who ruled out cardiac issues and sent him to the emergency room of our local hospital where he remained until he died three weeks later.

Diagnosis: Hamman-Rich syndrome is an acute and rapidly progressive form of cryptogenic fibrosing alveolitis of unknown aetiology. Both sexes affected; slight male predominance. Highest incidence between forty and seventy years of age. Fatal within weeks or months of onset.

Translation: The soft tissue in my father's lungs hardened very rapidly, making it difficult for him to breathe. No one knows why this happened. There were no treatment options. He died because his lungs turned to stone.

Hospitals are not good for much, but they are good for poetry. Shards of grief had tenderized me in such a way that the fragments and fronds of poetry suddenly made sense: *Oh, this is what it's for.* My hunt for lyric led me quickly to Rilke, someone I felt like I was supposed to have already read, stereotypical poet of all poets, a being for whom everything is a struggle, an undertaking, an *event.*

But for all of his apparent pretense, Rilke very genuinely occupied himself with the task of discovering and expressing something pure, the spaces in between his stanzas speaking truth. He was consumed with opposites, with grappling, climbing aboard the pendulum of feeling on which all human beings find themselves swinging. All at once, the despair and the soul-stirring joy, the fullness of the world. Expression for which there is no container. The abundance of life, the devastation of death; we will speak about this human condition as long as it is ours.

Rebecca chose photography first; breaking into abandoned buildings for their edges and light, shape and abstraction. Her work was spare and powerful, her standards for herself exacting. I sat for her as she shot dozens of photographs, collaging them into a giant composite pieces, experimenting with exposure, with contrast, with Sabatier. Then it was sculpture's turn, hours of welding, bending metal into compliance, the artist's will imbuing the substance.

Her mother's cancer danced back and forth: tumor index marker down, oh no, it has spiked again. At our college graduation, Karen's head was soft with duck fuzz, her eyelashes just sprouting back. Karen and her husband drove up to New England for the trees and mountains she had never seen. In Boston, she fainted because of fluid around her heart: fluid with cancer cells in it, like a glass of watermelon juice pocked with black seeds.

Rebecca moved home, spent long nights in the darkroom, in the studio, submitting applications to graduate school. Cancer came then into the lymph nodes. The doctors tried another drug: this one made Karen crawl on the floor in tears, her back on fire. Rebecca withdrew her applications, did dishes and laundry, drove to every chemo appointment, sent email updates with subjects such as "it's a very, very mad world" and sign-offs like "suck the marrow and live while you're alive."

Finally the fluid came back, and new masses appeared, in Karen's armpit, and along her neck. The doctors irradiated, but it only made them smaller. It did not make them disappear.

Christianity holds fast to Platonic dualism, as the Abrahamic faiths almost always do. *This* the realm of the body, flawed, polluted, and corrupted. *That* the realm of pure ideal, God's place, a state to which we can only hope our souls will be restored. *This* your earthly vehicle, flesh to be reviled. *That* your true self, made in the image of the divine. Hold onto one, disregard the other.

But it is difficult to disregard a body in rebellion. Difficult to believe that we indeed move beyond the earthly when the earthly is quickly slipping away. Hard to say what will be left when the flesh feels so real.

When I look at Rothko's early work, work for which he is not famous, work which does not really look like "his," I see an artist warming up, searching for an authentic form for his expression. Feeling is present, honest feeling, a kind of searching despair. And want. In the wake of one World War and in the midst of another, the world's artistic soil was volcanic—born of destruction, rich and ripe. Picasso, of course, had begun his famous manipulations with the human form, jolting the picture plane out of focus, amputating limbs and shattering anatomical structure. But Rothko wanted to portray the human form without "mutilating" it, as he felt Picasso was. Perhaps he thought that in the wake of the Second World War to fracture the human form was gratuitous, blasphemous even. What Rothko wanted was a new way to control and order experience in a time when he found himself and the world quite out of kilter.

Like many of his contemporaries, Rothko began to turn towards ancient mythologies and so-called "primitive" art for ways to express and even explain the constancy of the human condition. But that early work, though earnest in its intent and thoughtful in content, looks flat and unremarkable, like an imitation of someone else's style. Rothko knew that he was not achieving what he hoped, that something was being lost in translation from mind to page. So with great reluctance he made a radical choice; he stopped using any representations of the human form in his work.

The morning before I went to see *Red* on Broadway, I stood before a few other Rothkos—of the canvas variety—at the towering new

MoMa, glassy and stacked, fat-bellied with tourists. The paintings, two of my favorites, were nestled into an exhibit titled "The Modern Myth." Moving through the exhibit, I began to feel like its title was somewhat misleading, for I failed to see what our modern myth looks like, or, in fact, if it even exists at all.

Myth does not seem to come so naturally to us now as it did, it seems, to our ancient forebears. We are suspicious of anything that is eager or genuine, perhaps because we know too much. If one is conscious that one is making meaning, can one then no longer make it? Some would argue this is the result of science, that mythology has been replaced with a temple made of laboratories and reactors, with nodes for the brain, measuring waves.

But we humans still face "a sea of troubles," as Hamlet says, no matter how modern we have become. We are all heir to it, the shock and the heartache, the unexpected collateral damage, the proverbial slings and arrows. No amount of science, as powerful and necessary as it is in its own right, will ever undo that. Rothko eschewed what he called the "probable and familiar" human form, chose color and essence instead. Rilke looked back to an ancient story and made it his own. Perhaps our present-day myth just needs time to cure, to form a skin, a seal, a bubble of authority. Either that or we'll have to tear it all down and begin again.

Orpheus was a musician of unexcelled artistry. To him were conferred the distinct and unique honors of priesthood in the temples of both Apollo and Dionysus. He embodied the marriage of restraint and license, cerebral pleasures and earthly ones. Reconciliation of these dualities is impossible to quantify, but suffice it to say that Orpheus and his song brought solace and softness even to the hounds of hell.

In his account of Orpheus, Rilke gives us the pleasures of a wind-swept world, the taste of apples, and the fullness of love all made sweeter by the pang of death. Orpheus has seen the world, has charmed the creatures, has known loss, has wept. His grief transforms him. He inhabits his body but is not bound to it. He holds his life, at least according to Rilke, "open to death."

Be ahead of all parting, as though it already were
behind you, like the winter that has just gone by.
For among these winters there is one so endlessly winter
that only by wintering through it will your heart survive.
—Rainer Maria Rilke, *The Sonnets to Orpheus* II, 13

Meaning is immanent, the vehicle that binds. Rothko said, "For an artist, the problem is to talk about and do something outside yourself." To seek dissolution in a task, in the effort, is both the joy and the sacrifice. "Art is an adventure into an unknown world, which can only be explored by those willing to take the risks," he wrote. The artistic process is an Orphic descent.

Rebecca's father built the casket in which his wife was eventually buried. One fine January day, a sick-yet-still-living Karen stepped into that box, laid her frail, naked body down, and let her daughter capture her image. Karen folded one arm up against her chest, holding a crucifix in one hand, dark against her pale body. Red, worming scars and dark crosses made by doctors to indicate, *Irradiate here*, bloomed into the camera lens. Karen faced the camera as she had faced her whole life, without fear or pretense. As death brought them a distance, the whole was activated.

Rothko's chapel was built to be a place of self-confrontation and ultimately, transformation. "A theatre for the viewer," he called it, a theatre in which you are no longer the audience but the opening act. You stand on his stage, bare save the expanse of feeling laid out before you. Discover that painfully acute consciousness of the here and now, which the Christians call our "fallenness" and the Existentialists, our "angst."

Rothko felt what he called "the urgency for transcendent experience." He sought it for himself and he wanted, in his work as an artist, to provide it for others. Rothko believed that his work had the power to force viewers to directly confront their own temporality. Art had a purpose that the world could not contaminate, he believed that, even if he did not always believe that he was living up to that purpose.

The Rothko Chapel has been hailed as the greatest religious monument of our time. Its aesthetic as a sacred space is most often compared to that of a synagogue or a mosque: austere elegance, pared down and authentic. The chapel contains a few plain, black benches and meditation cushions, and the only ornamentation is that which Rothko was commissioned by John and Dominique deMenil to paint: fourteen giant panels which line the octagonal walls, over twelve feet in height.

The paintings were inspired by the Basilica of Santa Maria dell'Assunta on the island of Torcello in Italy. Torcello lies along the north part of the Venetian lagoon and its basilica, which dates back to 639 CE, is its only tourist attraction. While the exterior is somewhat plain, the basilica's interior shouts with the colors of elaborate mosaic work. On the western wall is a depiction of The Last Judgment, hellish and unflinching in its detail. In direct opposition, at the eastern end of the building stands a tiled representation of Madonna and child, as serene and lovely as the other wall is wretched.

This duality is mirrored in the design of the Rothko Chapel panels, one against the entrance wall, a black field, the other a triptych against the apse wall, lightened with a touch of purple. Death and resurrection face each other, "cancel the count." Where is this God of ours hidden? Hidden, perhaps, under layers of crimson and oxblood and blue. Hidden, perhaps, in our doubt and self-examination.

Available, perhaps, when we abandon the specificity of self. In Rothko's imagining of eternity, the whole is activated.

In July of 2006, Rebecca flies to my hometown to be with me for my father's funeral. She helps me cut, mount, and arrange family photographs in frames for display; she manages the print margins and folding of several hundred programs; she holds my weeping mother for me because I cannot, because I have to greet and thank the long line of people who have shown up to tell my father goodbye.

Eight months later, Rebecca flies out to visit me in Arizona, where I am completing graduate school, and we drive together to see the Grand Canyon and picnic on its rim. We imagine the horror and disbelief of the first human to behold such a thing. The brain, which cannot comprehend, decides: a devil, an enchantment, a mirage. We may deny, but we cannot escape our own insignificance.

We celebrate Rebecca's birthday on a sunny Sunday morning, complete with homemade biscuits and cheap, grad school-issue mimosas, and that night we dress up to go out to a fancy restaurant for dessert. The next morning, I wrangle my way through airline customer service and put an obscenely large amount of money on a credit card to buy a ticket that will get Rebecca back home earlier than planned, because we have received word that her mother is at the end.

A few days later, I fly to Rebecca's hometown and drive to the graveside service wearing the same dress I wore the day I buried my father. Under the shade of strong oak trees in a graveyard where Karen's ancestors have been interred for generations, I slip off my shoes and help Rebecca toss mounds of the rocky earth atop the coffin Karen had posed for pictures in just a few months before. Dirt under our fingernails and grass in our toes, two girls in black dresses tearing at the earth.

In the play *Red*, a fictionalized but believable Rothko tells his assistant:

"In the National Gallery in London there's a picture by Rembrandt called Belshazzar's Feast…It's an Old Testament story from Daniel: Belshazzar, King of Babylon is giving a feast and he blasphemes, so a divine hand appears and writes some Hebrew words on the wall as a warning…In the painting these words pulsate from the dark canvas like something miraculous…'Mene, Mene, Tekel, Upharsin.' … 'You have been weighed in the balance and have been found wanting.'"

When asked about the content of his chapel panels, Rothko invoked "the infinite eternity of death."

Through a reduction of form, a paring down, Rothko sought epiphanic confrontation, an intuitive grasp of the whole. (*Epiphanic*: relating to an appearance or manifestation, especially of a divine being.) Can't you hear the beat of angel wings, hollow and slow, like the blades of a helicopter warming up? Epiphany, an illuminating discovery, realization, or disclosure. Here in the chapel we have the universe contained, mirroring in on itself, replicating. Each moment is an abyss filled with possibilities of how to be. As my friend Nietzsche would say, now choose.

I fell in love with Rothko long before I knew anything about the man or his artistic process. His paintings are transcendent, like canvas touchstones or portals. The sensation is one of standing on a threshold, an opening onto something ancient or wild. I think the work is pure precisely because it has nowhere to go. And the chapel paintings are arguably the most powerful of all of Rothko's work: they emanate, they hum. If you close your eyes, you can still feel their presence, like that of sun on skin.

It is no secret that Rothko struggled throughout his life; the inner against the outer, the mind refusing the body, the world of the senses no match for the world of his intellect. I think these familiar dichotomies weigh more heavily on some of us than others. "As one sat with him in his studio," Dominique de Menil wrote, "[O]ne knew he was up against a supreme challenge."

Mark Rothko never saw his chapel dedicated or open to the public. He committed suicide on February 27, 1971. He was sixty-eight years old. Death is perhaps a different kind of failure of form, one which most of us do not choose for ourselves. The weight of meaning holds us to the ground, ties us tightly to the world of the flesh. But there is always the danger that our meanings will fail us, like lovers or lungs or belief.

Orpheus is said to have met his death at the hands of the Maenads, devotees of Dionysus who resented Orpheus' having given up the worship of all gods save Apollo. As he rose for his sun salutation one day, the blood-lusting, wine-drunk women tore him from limb to limb and tossed his body parts into the river. Orpheus, whose voice made even the stones move, was torn to pieces but his head was left intact, mouth still singing as he bobbed along. Sounds absurd, but then...

My father, too, we tossed into a river, his pieces somewhat smaller, ash and bits of bone. When I stand on the banks of the Mississippi now, I decide that he is there as I cautiously goat-step down the stone bank to get close enough to toss flowers into the water. We create our own mythologies, we attempt to remain open to death.

Never has grief been possessed,
never has love been learned,
and what removes us in death
is not revealed.
Only the song through the land
hallows and heals.
   —Rilke, *The Sonnets to Orpheus*, I, 19

At the close of *Red*, after two years of working together—dancing around canvases, arguing, pushing—Rothko has fired his assistant. Ken wonders what he's done wrong, but it isn't that; Rothko has finally seen something in Ken that means he can no longer justify keeping him around.

Rothko: You need to find your contemporaries and make your own world, your own life…You need to get out there now, into the thick of it, shake your fist at them, talk their ear off…Okay?

Ken: Okay. *Beat.* Thank you.

Rothko: Make something new.

Nietzsche once described the artistic temperament as "a mystic soul almost undecided whether it should communicate or conceal itself." Our impetus to make things beautiful exists because we know that we will die. Because everything we love will die, too. What else should we do but scrabble on walls and tell stories? Creativity and mortality are inextricably linked. We are still figuring out what it means to be human; we scale life around death too often, not often enough.

Life and terror go hand in hand. In the communion with darkness, there must be an immersion. Orpheus, prepared to cross over, could activate the whole. Because he can let go, he is free. The dichotomies resolve. Our sorrows become vehicles of light.

Sources

Ashton, Dore. *About Rothko*. New York: Oxford UP, 1983. Print.

Beyeler, Fondation, ed. *Mark Rothko: Mark Rothko, «A Consummated Experience between Picture and Onlooker»* Ostfildern-Ruit: Hatje Cantz, 2001. Print.

Breslin, James E. B., and Mark Rothko. *Mark Rothko: A Biography*. Chicago: University of Chicago, 1993. Print.

Casey, Timothy J. *A Reader›s Guide to Rilke›s Sonnets to Orpheus*. Galway: Arlen House, 2001. Print.

Clearwater, Bonnie. "Shared Myths: Reconsideration of Rothko's and Gottlieb's Letter to *The New York Times*." *Archives of American Art Journal* 24.1 (1984): 23-25. Print.

De Menil, Dominique. «The Rothko Chapel.» *Art Journal* 30.3 (Spring 1971): 249-51. Print.

Lautermilch, Steven. «Rilke›s Orpehus: The Twin Kingdoms.» *Pacific Coast Philology* 12 (October 1978): 36-43. Print.

Nodelman, Sheldon. *The Rothko Chapel Paintings: Origins, Structure, Meaning*. Austin: University of Texas, 1997. Print.

Polcari, Stephen. "Mark Rothko: Heritage, Environment, and Tradition." *American Art* 2.2 (Spring 1988): 32-63. Print.

Rilke, Rainer Maria. *The Sonnets to Orpheus*. Trans. Stephen Mitchell. New York: Simon and Schuster, 1985. Print.

Selz, Peter Howard. *Mark Rothko*. New York: Museum of Modern Art, 1961. Print.

Acknowledgments

This book has been many years in the making, and would never have come to fruition without the love and unfailing support of so many incredible friends. Courtney Taylor Humphreys, Rebecca Villarreal, David Berry, Marynelle Wilson, Katherine & Stephen Bush, Megan Batchelor, and Phil Imus—you are my embarrassment of riches.

I am indebted to Arianne Zwartjes, Cara Blue Adams, Lauren Eggert-Crowe, and Alison Deming for their willingness to vouch for this book. I also owe thanks to the many readers who offered valuable feedback on previous incarnations of these essays, especially Liz Bender & Mikie Rath.

To Allie Mounce, who designed the most beautiful cover and interior art for this book, thank you.

I have been blessed in my life to have many fine teachers; I think that is why I became one. Without them, I would not be who I am today.

To anyone who has left a comment or note of encouragement on Blue Jean Gourmet over the last few years: thank you for being such a kind and lovely audience.

To Courtney Rath: I am forever indebted to your discerning editorial eye and generous spirit. I love you big much.

To my mom: you have generously shared stories and whispered encouragement in my ear for three decades now. I truly hope this book is worthy of you.

To Jill: you are my key, my partner, the source of so much strength, inspiration, and deep, abiding love. My gratitude to you and for you is boundless.

And finally, my Shiv: I always thought I would write a book first, then become a parent. But it turns out that I needed you in order to finish this. Thanks, baby. Mama thinks you're awesome.

Nishta J. Mehra is a fan of big conversations and good food. She spends her days working to figure out what it means to live fully and joyfully: as a mother, teacher, writer, daughter, friend, and spouse. Born and raised in Memphis, Tennessee, she lives with her partner Jill and their son Shiv in a suburb of Houston, Texas. Find more of her writing on her blog, Blue Jean Gourmet: www.bluejeangourmet.com

Made in the USA
Charleston, SC
18 September 2013